NAVIGATE

The Executive Leadership Journey

Part 1

Casey Kroll

With thanks to Becky Kroll for her hard work and perseverance in editing and offering great feedback.

Copyright © 2015--2019 Casey Kroll, Judi Williams, Rahul Dogra, Dale Darley
All rights reserved.
ISBN-13:978-1499277456
ISBN-10:1499277458

Foreword

Four authors with one common purpose seized an opportunity to share a legacy – and this book was conceived between them. The first seeds of the idea originated from the work of one of the authors.

Back in October 2011 Casey Kroll, a US-based business leader, consultant, author and training programme instructor, submitted his successful response to a senior level training programme called 'Preparing for Executive Leadership' call for proposals. The technical editorship was offered to his UK-based colleague, executive coach and author, Judi Williams. Developing the course was a unique and bonding experience for them both – they recounted their stories, shared experiences and best practices, debated and deliberated extensively and laughed even more.

As Casey launched the programme in the US for Learning Tree, Judi and another executive coach and author, Dale Darley, simultaneously rolled it out in the UK. The programme was an immense success and gained immediate positive feedback. Indeed, these first cohorts brought together through the programme are still active and sharing their journeys today. Rahul Dogra, a business strategist, author, coach and consultant was brought onto the team as an additional facilitator to meet the expected growth in demand.

They had so much positive feedback from the participants, and fun delivering it, that they felt that a product as good as this deserved to be expanded and shared, and so 'Navigate', as conceived by Casey and Judi, was developed and born with additional perspectives and contributions from Dale and Rahul.

The synergy between them was obvious, as they collaborated, inspired and motivated each other to take the initial ideas and create a comprehensive tool kit that would inspire, guide, motivate and support anyone in or preparing for a role in Executive Leadership.

In the beginning, they were simply four individual writers. As the project progressed, they became a writing team – discovering that their blend of cultures, experiences and perspectives created valuable new insights and brought a certain balance to their collective work. They learned from each other, and from the experience of co-authoring itself.

We invite you to absorb the differences in style and voice and use them to judge how you might best flex your leadership voice to communicate, inspire, engage and motivate those who can deliver your success. It is through creating the context within which your followers will be successful, that your executive leadership success can ultimately be achieved.

This book and the supporting workbook and journal contain that framework for your Executive Leadership development plan, a roadmap for their journey, and a measurement tool for your progress.

Legal Notices

No part of this publication may be reproduced or transmitted in any material form (including photocopying or storing it in any medium by electronic means) without the written permission of the authors.

The purpose of this book is to educate, entertain and provide information on the subject matter covered. All attempts have been made to verify information at the time of this publication, and the authors do not assume any responsibility for errors, omissions or other interpretations of the subject matter. The purchaser or reader of this book assumes responsibility for the use of this material and information. The authors assume no responsibility or liability on behalf of any purchaser or reader of this book.

Table of Contents

The Executive Leadership Journey 1
Plan Journeys 13
Know Yourself 27
Understand The Business 43
Create Vision 59
Strike Balances 75
Lead Strategies 93
Make Connections 117
Build Trust 129
Taking Stock 153
About the Authors 155
Bibliography 161

THE EXECUTIVE LEADERSHIP JOURNEY

Casey Kroll

The Executive Leadership Journey

This book is quite different from all other books related to leadership development. This is because it is unique in its focus on the Executive Leadership journey: the journey to, and the journey of Executive Leadership guided by the sixteen key points of the Executive Leadership compass. We define Executive Leadership to be the leadership that must be exercised by any person, at any level within an organisation who desires to be or currently is, entrusted to steer the organisation. It very importantly extends to guiding themselves and their organisation through tomorrow's challenges.

Executive Leadership goes well beyond the common areas of personal leadership attributes and skills. It uniquely includes that special additional leadership knowledge, experiences, traits, behaviours and skills required for success in the journey to, and in continued occupancy of, a seat on the Executive Leadership team of any organisation

We do this because executive leaders in all organisations have special stature and importance, not just for themselves, but also for the current and future health of the entire organisation. This, in turn, affects its staff and other stakeholders, including investors, donors / contributors, customers, clients and even its suppliers and the environment within which it operates.

When I was approximately eight years old, and experiencing the sudden loss of my paternal grandmother, my father shared a very powerful view of life with me. First, he asked me to rejoice in the fact that I had had a chance to know her, for he had never known his grandparents. He went on to say that one of his mother's lessons to him was that for each of us, when we were born, our eventual date of passing was also determined. In closing, he shared that we obviously do not know when that will occur. That it was up to each of us to do the best that we can in the time, we have in between those two dates.

In doing our best, we often have to change and to adapt to changing circumstances: circumstances in our lives, the lives of our loved ones, and in the environment of our organisations. In continuing his lesson to me, my father emphasized that we must do our best under these conditions; that we must not just tolerate change; we must optimize it, and embrace it. Additionally, we need to help others around us to do so as well.

Yes, we, who are in or are seeking Executive Leadership positions, must do more than embrace change that is thrust upon us. We must maximize the results of change by setting destinations, charting the courses, and mustering the troops. By doing so, we ensure that we personally, and our organisation, maximize the multi-dimensional goals that we have help set.

Organisations of all types look to senior executive leaders for multi-dimensional leadership. The specific areas include but are not limited to the common personal traits associated with leadership such as authenticity and integrity. They also look to Executive Leaders to guide the organisation in setting and fulfilling its mandate or mission, including its strategic direction, integrity, innovation, relevance, etc.

The Executive Leadership Journey

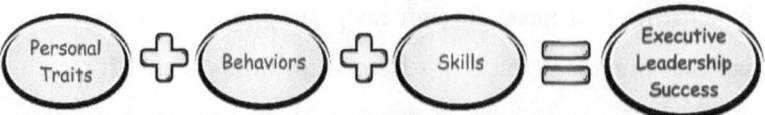

Simply put, one cannot be a successful Executive Leader and either produce or lead a failed or failing organisation. For example, it is one thing to ensure that we personally have integrity, but it is another thing to ensure that the organisation we lead, and the individuals within it, also operate with integrity.

Therefore, when exploring the many facets of Executive Leadership, we will be focusing on personal leadership as the core. Then on extending the traits, skills and behaviours required of executive leaders to ensure the comprehensive health of the organisation they help lead.

The path to success at the Executive Leadership level is often a long, potentially strenuous journey. Like Olympic athletes attaining the medals podium, one does not usually find themselves in a position of Executive Leadership by accident. It may have been or will be, a long journey, a strenuous journey, not in the directions originally anticipated. It may have been and will continue to be, a journey with many pitfalls. But it is one with potentially many rewards for oneself, for one's family, for one's organisation and even for the community at large.

As executive leaders, we must derive additional energy and focus from our successes, and from our dealings with any setbacks that will arise along our path. If you do not do so already, it is imperative that you learn how to do this. This resiliency, in both our interrelated personal and professional lives, helps us, and those around us, accomplish more, with less effort.

Many more attempt the journey to Executive Leadership than navigate it well. Many who succeed in attaining their goal of Executive Leadership do less than competent jobs at fulfilling the numerous essential roles required of an executive leader. It is a journey that you may do alone, or at least at times feel as if you are doing it alone. No more! You now have support in navigating your Executive Leadership journey.

Our communal goals in this book and its related tools are to help you navigate your Executive Leader journey. To help you in your quest of the personal traits, behaviours and skills needed for success as an Executive Leader. And to help you maximize your experiences and lessons learned along your journeys.

Our concept of navigation of any journey has three essential and complementary elements

- To ascertain, or plot and control, a course of action
- To move or progress in a logical sequence, and to
- To 'find one's way'

One of the false paradoxes of this comprehensive view of navigation is that despite the planning and preparation that one may do prior to a journey one often finds themselves with the necessity of having to just 'find one's way'.

That pre-work has not been for nought. By contrast, it has been a valuable investment in the future. It provides us with essential foundations, understandings, preparations and insights that enable and improve our abilities to improvise, adapt, adjust and overcome, within timeframes that support our continuing journey.

You may be reading this book out of curiosity, to benchmark your Executive Leadership abilities, to strengthen one or more existing skills or to develop a comprehensive Executive Leadership program. Introspection and self-assessment are a necessary foundation for growth. From these to some greater or lesser degree, a purposeful series of self-development initiatives occur.

SELF AWARENESS AND INTROSPECTION: THE FOUNDATIONS OF PERSONAL GROWTH

We are all products of our personal experiences, the knowledge we have obtained, the stories we have heard and the heroes and heroines we have had the privilege of encountering. We can passively let these foundations of ourselves be ourselves, or we can recognize and then play a larger role in shaping ourselves.

Life is not about 'discovering' ourselves …
It is about inventing and crafting ourselves

To invent, or craft ourselves, whether as the passive result of happenstance or as the focused choices of our consciousness, brings the inevitability of dealing with change, potentially large change.

One of the benefits of 'self-inflicted change' is that it can be easier to accept than change that is thrust upon us. None the less, change is change, and it does not happen easily.

In order to first, even have the desire to craft ourselves in some purposeful way, and then to determine the appropriate courses of action to take, requires a combination of introspection, self-awareness and desire.

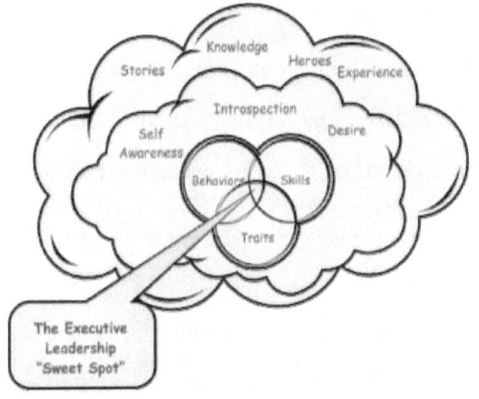

This book guides you through this process of introspection and self-awareness, reinforcing your desire to incorporate appropriate behaviours, skills and traits.

OUR COMPREHENSIVE EXECUTIVE LEADERSHIP GUIDE AND PLANNING SYSTEM

As with any journey, it is essential to bring along the right kit, and to have a navigation system appropriate to the task at hand, in order to minimize the number of wrong turns taken.

Our communal goal is to provide you with that comprehensive navigation system for the introspection, self-assessment and plan-full development of your Executive Leadership journeys.

Historically, for navigation, a good compass and a good road map were essential tools. Today, many set out on physical journeys with their trusty (or not so trusty) electronic GPS system. These combine the functionality of a compass with scalable mapping, routing, and 'points-of-interest'.

The Executive Leadership Journey

To assist you on your Executive Leadership journeys, we have developed a comprehensive set of tools for you, essentially a fully integrated GPS system for your Executive Leadership journeys, *the Executive Leadership Guide and Planning System* (Executive Leadership GPS). This Executive Leadership GPS is composed of three interrelated elements.

1. **The Executive Leadership Compass** which identifies the 16 key guideposts on the journey to Executive Leadership. It includes the traits, skills, tools and techniques needed for a successful journey, much like the 16 major points of a navigation compass, to help you navigate your journey.

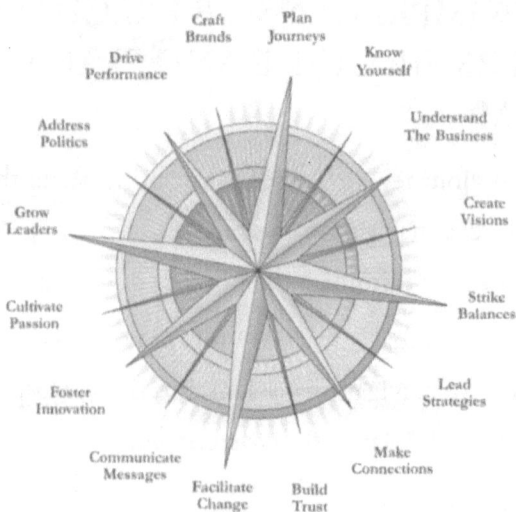

Each of these 16 compass points has benefit in and of itself as a stand-alone guidepost along your journey. Additionally, each of these is interrelated, and synergistic, with one or more of the other 16 Compass points. It is through this synergy that the power of our Compass really comes to bear, for leaders and most importantly, for the unique demands on Executive Leadership

2. **The Executive Leadership Road Map,** a scalable self-assessment and prioritization tool, for now, and for the future. It will guide you and help you visualize your evolving Executive Leadership development status, needs and accomplishments.

Rating		Rating system: Choose the appropriate guidelines for scoring each entry					
3 = Highly relevant now and in future 2 = Relevant now or in future 1 = Not relevant now but *is* in future 0 = Not relevant now, nor in the future	Development phase: My current level of expertise	Phase 0: May know or have heard of concept, but lacks any training or experience.	Phase 1: Has formal training or education. Understands the concept.	Phase 2: Can apply learning to the personal workplace.	Phase 3: Applies the knowledge in the context of direct supervisor, coworker, team member, etc.	Phase 4: More complex application of the concepts to broad, nonhomogenous groups. It is now part of your	Phase 5: Routinely applies concept without need for conscious thought. A core part of your vision, principles, and both subordinate and
	How much like me?	Not at all	Very little	Little	Some	Much	Very much
	Points	0	1	2	3	4	5
Relevance to your situation 0 to 3	Current capability rating 0 to 5	Urgency 3 = Immediate 2 = Short-term 1 = Long-term					

The scalable, comprehensive Road Map guides you through an assessment of your current interests, needs and priorities. Then it guides you, step by step, to develop a comprehensive self-development plan, with both near term and long term 'way points'. You will have access to several formats of our Executive Leadership Road Map with its key points-of-interest via download from https://daledarley.com/my-executive-leadership.

It is designed to be applied throughout your journey to Executive Leadership, and for those ongoing journeys that you take as an Executive Leader.

3. **Your Executive Leadership Journal,** a multi-format,

customizable journal specifically focused to help you record your ongoing thoughts, insights, impressions and commitments gathered along your journey. As with the Road Map, the multiple formats of Your Executive Leadership Journal are available for download at https://daledarley.com/my-executive-leadership/. Journaling is one of the most powerful and effective ways to clarify your thoughts. We encourage you to buy a journal or to use a computer-based one and write daily. Find the right time of day to read this book and the use your journal to record whatever comes up for you. Create your perfect reading, journaling and reflecting environment. A few days after you have journaled, read what you have written, let the thoughts come, these are your "aha!" moments. Reflect and decide what to do. Take your time; this is your journey.

Each of these interrelated tools can be used alone. However, their real power, as with a GPS navigation system, comes from the synergy of the component parts: the 16 Point Compass, the

Roadmap with Way-Points, and your Journal to guide and record your introspection and evolution as an Executive Leader.

CHECK YOUR PROGRESS

The journey of Executive leadership is not a quick one. Take time, every chapter or two, to check your progress. Review Your Executive Leadership Journal and the entries you have made in your Roadmap to Executive Leadership. If you are not following the book in a linear fashion, this is particularly useful, as when you flick through you can see what you have read and actioned.

Now it is time to get started!

We all, Casey, Judi, Rahul and Dale, wish you productive and rewarding journeys!

PLAN JOURNEYS

Casey Kroll

Alice: "Would you tell me, please, which way I ought to go from here?"
The Cat: "That depends a good deal on where you want to get to".
Alice: "I don't much care where".
The Cat: "Then it doesn't much matter which way you go".
Alice: "...so long as I get somewhere".
The Cat: "Oh, you're sure to do that, if only you walk long enough".
From Alice in Wonderland

Plan Journeys

Like an Olympic athlete attaining the medals podium, one does not usually find one's self in a position of Executive Leadership within an organisation by accident. The path to success at this level is often a long, potentially strenuous journey. It is an evolving journey with many pitfalls and obstacles, but also one with many rewards: for the individual, for their family, for the organisation and even for the community at large.

It is most likely that we are simultaneously pursuing multi-dimensional journeys crossing and intertwining multiple segments of our being – personal, family, friends, our profession and the organisation we help lead. These are not likely to all end well if they are 'by accident' as opposed to 'on purpose'. They require planning, multi-dimensional planning, in order to address the often competing demands of our multi-faceted existence: ourselves, our family and friends, our organisations...

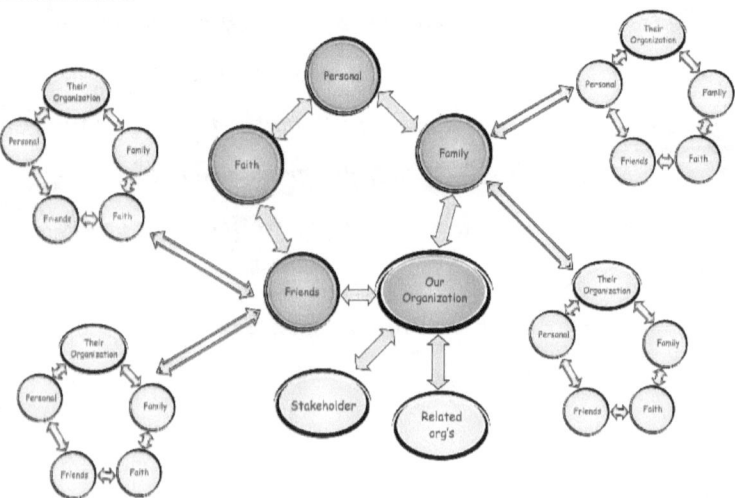

One must also remember that even with the best planning

imaginable, one cannot anticipate all potential circumstances. Therefore, we must be ready and willing to adapt or to modify both our goals and our paths to them. Knowing when to do this is the essential difference between perseverance and stubbornness.

Our journeys are in some regards journeys without end; quests. As one accomplishes personal, family, professional and organisation goals seldom do true leaders say "I have arrived. My work is done!"

We are more likely to take a period of reflection, and possibly rest. Then at some point, begin to examine what has yet to be achieved or the next fork in the road, and set out again. The new quests may be to higher levels of achievement or development within the same realms. They may be along forks in the roads to all new realms. In either case, once again we set our goals, determine our strategies and plan our journeys.

WHAT IS PLANNING?

Because of the many aspects and complexity of the path to Executive Leadership, via our selected strategies with specific goals, a sound travel plan is essential, both for us personally and for our organisation.

Planning journeys occurs at many levels. Planning includes, much like a series of navigation charts, a full range of perspectives. These range from the highest, broadest most comprehensive view to detailed routing through a complex maze of desired waypoints and dead-ends (closes) and hazards. The plans for our journeys require ongoing assessment, adaptation and reaction to new and ever evolving circumstances, much like the navigators on the ships of exploration as they crossed the oceans.

Planning journeys includes more than just setting a route to our goal or destination; it includes identifying the necessary actions, determining the necessary resources, and estimating the costs and the timing of our actions. And, as mentioned briefly above, the possibility of a comprehensive reassessment of the goals and paths outlined due to new or evolving circumstances.

There are many thousands of books and articles on how to plan: how to plan our vacations, finances, projects, and even how to plan making a plan. The single most important criterion for success is to have a planning process. Define that process, apply that process, assess its effectiveness and improve it as needed to ensure that you can effectively achieve those goals that you have established for yourself, for your family and for your organisation.

As you, your family and your organisation grow and evolve your approach to planning will by necessity, evolve.

To help you do this necessary planning, I provide a very simple, minimal model of the required characteristics of any plan in the section below titled 'How to do it?'. It is a good starting point and serves as a good reminder to you of the most basic steps to take along your personal and professional journey in Executive Leadership.

WHY BOTHER?

Without the investment of the time and effort to develop a well thought out plan, we will be woefully unprepared to deal with the all-too-certain parade of unanticipated events and circumstances that keep us from achieving our goals.

> *"In preparing for battle I have always found that plans are useless, but planning is indispensable."* Dwight D. Eisenhower
> *(Military Leader and Politician)*

Additionally, as an Executive Leader, both our personal, professional and organisational development plans affect and are affected by, others. Without planning, there cannot be coordination of the plans to enable and foster synergy and to reduce conflict and miscommunication. As Executive Leaders, we need to avoid these consequences. We have a responsibility to ourselves, to our organisations and to others that we impact, to plan effectively. In turn, in order to plan effectively, one must have an understanding of themselves and the business, one must have strategies, build visions, strike balance: in short, the entire executive leadership compass. Planning journeys, depending on their nature, may be a solo activity, or it may be a team sport with you holding one of the most important seats: responsible for leading the planning of the journey.

HOW TO DO IT?

Planning can take many forms. I like to go back to my earliest days as a professional, and a poster I once saw in my manager's office. I do not recall its exact content or its source, but the gist of the message is that there are major differences between ideas and plans. Many years ago, I created my personal version of that poster to serve as a constant reminder and to coach myself as well as others. It is wonderful to have a good idea, but it is essential to turn those good ideas into coordinated actions in order to ensure that the idea becomes a reality.

THERE IS A HUGE DIFFERENCE	
An Idea	A Plan
In one's head	In writing
Limited involvement from other parties	Participation from involved and impacted parties
Vague objectives, superlatives (best, better, more, most, sooner, …)	Specific, measurable goals
Non-specific time-frame (soon, ASAP, …)	Specific time-frames
Vague, non-measurable results (faster, improved, …)	Measurable results
No final report card	Auditable results tracked against the goals, supporting continuous process improvement

Each of these elements of 'A Plan', when applied to our ideas, helps to ensure the successful realization of the idea, both for us in our personal journeys and for the organisations, we lead.

Navigate

By committing our ideas to writing, we create substance that can be analysed, reviewed, edited and improved upon, honing the idea and helping it to grow.

By including those accompanying us in our journeys and those touched by our journeys, we can more easily identify shortcomings, obstacles and creative implementations, and overcome resistance to change. We can foster creativity and invention in determining approaches, or even the goals themselves. We can identify areas where our ideas are not congruent with those held by some or all within the organisation. We can develop our courses of action at the earliest possible time as opposed to having to react to these discoveries at a later date. Very importantly, we must scale the level of others' involvement based on numerous factors such as degree of impact, influence and power to name just a few.

By developing specific and measurable goals, we can assess the benefits that we expect and weigh them against the efforts and risks that we are taking to achieve them. They provide focus and purpose. Additionally, many of us, our cohorts and our followers are motivated by achievement and developing these measurable goals helps motivate us to achieve them.

By establishing specific time-frames we maintain focus and an appropriate sense of urgency. Research shows that the accomplishment of specific goals within specific timeframes is a key motivator to many. Too long of a time frame contributes to the loss of focus; too short leads to frustration and burn-out.

By having clearly measurable results, we can determine our

Plan Journeys

progress, evaluate the effectiveness of our actions, and make corrections and modifications to bring us back on course. In most instances, it would be laughable to undertake even a simple holiday road trip without knowing the distance to be covered and then measuring progress against it. This approach would hamper the proper execution of routes and the obtaining of nourishment and lodging along the way. Why would we embark on a career journey or lead our organisation on a journey without similar ongoing measures to ensure progress toward our anticipated results?

Lastly, and potentially of greatest value due to its building upon the previous ones, by having auditable results, reported against our goals, we openly determine the true degree to which we have attained our plan. This open assessment can help us determine the areas where we excelled and the ones where we need further development. It can motivate us and organisation's teams to achieve. It creates a record, unblemished by time and the inevitable recasting of the results by dimmed memories. Additionally, recognition that eventually this accounting will be done can have a tempering effect on the pursuit of fool-hardy initiatives, or goals. Auditing our progress, and more importantly, our evolving capabilities, knowledge, tools, understandings and insights, provides feedback for our course corrections and our goal modifications. When we fail at this step, we leave ourselves and our organisation prone to habitually repeating the same errors.

To invest the time and the effort to convert ideas to plans

forces higher levels of effort and concentration. This, in turn, fosters higher levels of thought and understanding that can allow us to appear spontaneously brilliant in our adaptation to changing or new developments.

The rigour and level of detail of plans for any given journey must be tailored to the aspects of the journey. A shopping trip to the local town centre for groceries may be planned very casually, without much structure. However, a large, annual trip to stock up on rare or special items may require more in-depth and thorough effort.

A bit of a dichotomy can emerge here, for, the more experienced we are with any particular journey, the less rigorous our planning tends to be. For familiar journeys, our detailed plans would be very sound as they are based on considerable understanding of the territory. However, detailed planning may not be worth the effort. We instead rely on our own experience and on that of our organisation. We adopt minimalistic formal plans if any at all. With new journeys to uncharted waters, which can have the largest hazards and therefore need careful planning, we often do not have enough of the knowledge, skills, insights and experience to plan well. In these circumstances, the most common ways to address this gap are through targeted research, development, experimentation and coaching from trusted advisors for us, our organisation and even our families. Often this is coupled with iterative plans, each building upon the experiences recently gained.

When these approaches are not possible, and we believe

Plan Journeys

that the journey is worth taking, along with its associated risks, building our knowledge and experience through pioneering may the only alternative. For some, these are the only journeys worth pursuing, and for others, they are journeys to be avoided.

I did not know it at the time, but in retrospect, I learned that one of my first and best lessons in project management came literally at my mother's knee. She used to read to me, my sister and my brother. As she read, she would share the segments of an orange. Her readings were mostly nursery rhymes and fairy tales. I remember, in particular, the story of Goldilocks and the Three Bears. I often use this story when I am helping project managers develop the skills necessary for their success in that very challenging arena.

The best lesson to me from this experience with my mother was to look beyond the immediate gratification of the orange segments, for the power of the tales being told. Goldilocks discovered that one of the chairs was too big, one too small and one just right. She found one bowl of porridge too hot, one too cold and one just right. Lastly, she found one bed too hard, one too soft and the last one just right. Choosing an answer or solution to a challenge is important, choosing an answer that fits the circumstances is more important.

Our approach to planning is very similar in that we must use enough rigour to accomplish our journey successfully. Not just the 'size' but also the complexity is important.

Too   much

planning and we waste time on planning versus doing. We demotivate our most experienced, capable and insightful associates. We needlessly delay the start of our journeys. We waste money creating something of more detail than is needed.

Plan Journeys

Too little planning and we spend excessive effort reacting to events and circumstances that could have and should have been foreseen. We fail to accomplish our goals and demotivate our best associates because of frustration and rework, correcting avoidable errors and backtracking.

Goldilocks had this one right – not too much, not too little, just right; an easy lesson to give, but a difficult one to apply.

WHAT IF WE DON'T DO IT?

Without 'A Plan', anyone is subject to distraction and diversion by short term events. Often these distracting events are urgent but may be of low overall importance. They continually redirect our efforts, divert us from our Executive Leadership journey, and prevent us from attaining the more important personal, professional and organisational goals we that we seek.

Relying only on 'An Idea' of a journey to Executive Leadership deprives us of important tools and assistance. Developing 'A Plan', in writing, with the assistance of the other affected parties, including specific goals and milestones with measurable results, allows us to audit our progress and to make mid-course corrections. Without 'A Plan' that is developed and implemented in consort with the other affected parties, we deprive ourselves of the ability to remove obstacles before they materialize. Additionally, and very importantly, we deprive ourselves of the ability to lower resistance to change.

Navigate

POINTS OF INTEREST

Some of the key facets of this chapter include:

- **Enlisting participation:** How often, and how well, do you enlist those accompanying you, or touched by your journeys, in the planning of the journeys?

- **Setting specific, measurable goals:** How well-versed are you at developing effective, specific, measurable goals to provide clarity of purpose and to help motivate achievement?

- **Establishing specific time-frames:** Do you know how to set appropriate timelines for your and others' advantage? Are they realistic? Are they aligned with priorities? Do they support the vision?

- **Measuring results:** Do you know how to effectively and efficiently measure progress, sufficiently to be of true value, without bias, and without placing an undue burden on yourself or your organisation? Do you hold regular, meaningful reviews to gauge progress?

- **Auditing results to support process improvement:** Do you know how to establish constructive audits that feed continual improvement? Do you routinely use them for self-assessment and progress checks? Do you employ audits within your organisation, constructively, to aid growth and development, to identify areas in need of improvement and to share best practices throughout your organisation?

Plan Journeys

Remember as you read through the chapter to reflect on the questions asked, note what comes up in your journal. Use the resources we have made available to you to check and assess where you are. Following reflection, witness what comes up for you and make a note of that and any actions required.

KNOW YOURSELF

Judi Williams

"Authenticity in a leader is crucial. Followers will not commit if they do not trust you and believe that you have integrity."
Kevin Murray

Know Yourself

The most successful leaders that I have worked with shared certain qualities – they knew themselves well; they believed in lifelong learning; they wanted to be the best they could be; had passion, a strong sense of purpose, and they lived their values. They took action to understand who they were, what values and beliefs they held, what strengths and talents they possessed, and what resources they had within themselves that they could draw on (knowledge, acquired skills and competencies). Having achieved a reasonable measure of self-awareness, they then worked hard to develop their resources, and to seek out the environment within which they could use these to best advantage, for themselves, the organisation, and its stakeholders. Working with these leaders in the early stages of my career confirmed my values, shaped my views about Executive Leadership and eventually drew me into coaching others at this level.

It is imperative that your journey is inspired by a strong personal identity and a sense of purpose for yourself as an Executive Leader. In this chapter, I will be addressing the starting point of your journey to Executive Leadership. (Later chapters will discuss your vision and passion for your role.) Your journey is not about moving to a different place; rather it is growing into the person you want to be – your best self as an Executive Leader.

Your journey has to start with knowing *who you are now*, and identifying *who you could be*, at your best. This means being able to envisage yourself at a future time, recognising the resources you already have, knowing what you need to achieve, and then seeing and feeling yourself achieving your vision.

I will describe what 'authentic leadership' means; why it is vital to reflect on and come to understand who you are and demonstrate yourself authentically; how to achieve greater depth of self-knowledge and who can help you to do this. I'll help you identify the benefits of knowing and growing, and I'll discuss what could happen if you overlook the importance of self-knowledge and purposeful on-going self-development.

WHAT IS AUTHENTIC LEADERSHIP?

> *"To thine own self be true."* – Polonius,
> William Shakespeare's *Hamlet*

What makes a great leader? A multitude of notable and wise writers, commentators and researchers have addressed this question from many perspectives throughout history. Views differ about whether great leadership emanates from what you have, what you do or who you are.

The late, great Stephen Covey suggested that theories of leadership that focus on traits, styles or innate qualities *"have had more explanatory rather than predictive value"* and in my experience, this is certainly the case. He suggests *"A more fruitful approach is to look at followers, rather than leaders, and to assess leadership by asking why followers follow."*

From my personal experience, we tend to follow a leader when we share their strong sense of purpose, where we trust and respect that person because we find them authentic. We find them credible individuals with a coherent vision and a passion for the future that connects emotionally with others. *(Create Visions, Cultivate Passion)*

There is no fixed formula for great Executive Leadership, and no single set of characteristics or behaviours that I subscribe to. Possessing specific traits does not necessarily translate directly into great Executive Leadership. I believe that we all possess the potential to be a great leader in our unique way; by discovering our uniqueness within, connecting to it and by maximizing it Executive Leaders can become the best that they can be.

Consideration of the answer should start with the question "What is the purpose of Executive Leadership?" Theorists through the decades have more or less agreed on this aspect – Executive Leadership is about creating the future and then encouraging those who will deliver it through their passion for the vision. I consider that Executive Leaders in today's increasingly complex world must create an environment within which others can be the best that they can be - where the individuals and organisations that they lead can learn, develop, adapt and grow, and sustain themselves into the future.

Over the last couple of decades, growing importance has been attributed to the more 'human' side of leadership and the emotional impact on others of what a senior leader says and does. Leaders who demonstrate language and behaviours that are 'emotionally resonant' are more successful in inspiring, motivating and igniting passion in followers than those who create 'dissonance' and don't connect with potential followers at the heart level. It is true to say that title or position in an organisation does not make a leader. It may give that person an opportunity, but leaders, and particularly Executive Leaders, are affirmed in that role only when others choose to follow where they lead. It is active and willing followership that marks an effective Executive Leader.

HOW DO I BUILD SELF-KNOWLEDGE?

"All I can do is be me, whoever that is."

Bob Dylan

Great leadership starts with a desire to discover one's innate leader within, connecting to our inner wisdom; then exploring and reflecting at a deep level to understand what drives us, our values, our unique talents and strengths, and of what we are (and could be) capable. When we unlock our authentic leader within, we make better choices about how we actualize our leadership and connect credibly to the world and people around us.

In 'The Gifts of Imperfection' Brene Brown says, *"Authenticity is the daily practice of letting go of who we think we are supposed to be and embracing who we are."*

These values and beliefs drive my executive coaching practice and explain why I include in this chapter models, tools and techniques that will help you, the developing Executive Leader, to focus on your inner self and personal mastery. It is vitally important that you know who you are because leading others and contributing to the leadership of an organisation begins with leading oneself; therefore self-knowledge must be the starting point. Without self-knowledge, we lack the self-awareness vital for self-management, self-development and growth. We cannot change what we are not aware of. When we start with ourselves, and understand our unique map of the world, we are better able to relate to the maps of others, and appreciate the differences. Only when leaders recognise this can they work towards greater awareness of what makes them who they are.

There are many psychometric instruments, profiling tools and self-assessments that can help to build self-knowledge and awareness, and these are easily accessed from proprietary sources and commercial vendors. However, the more useful ones usually benefit from a qualified facilitator's feedback and explanation. Expert guidance through the results of the in-depth instruments will assist us to use the results to grow from, by understanding that they are useful as a tool for insight and self-knowledge, rather than to put an individual into a particular 'box' or 'type.'

Many contemporary organisations invite aspiring leaders to attend a Leadership Assessment Centre. Here they will work within a cohort of their peers to assess their strengths through various methods such as self-assessment, observation by assessors, group work and structured interviews. If this is available to you, I whole-heartedly encourage you to take advantage of the opportunity. Alternatively, you may find that your company can offer other personalised approaches to support you.

Maybe your organisation offers access to Executive Leadership development programmes or access to an internal coach who will work with you on a one-to-one basis. Alternatively, perhaps they may be open to sponsoring an external coach who is qualified to coach at the executive level.

HOW DO I CONTINUE MY PERSONAL GROWTH?

"It is never too late to be what you might have been."
George Eliot

With greater self-knowledge comes the ability to change and transform, and the insight to help others to do the same. There are many ways to develop our leadership competencies, such as:

- Self-paced discovery
- Volunteering
- On the job challenges
- Mentoring others and being mentored yourself
- Asking for feedback
- Personal reflection and journaling
- Finding new ways to do things
- Attending training for specific skills or competencies
- Working with an executive coach

Executive Leadership coaching provides the optimum platform for leadership self-awareness and the alignment of personal and organisational values.

Know Yourself

John Whitmore, the renowned writer and authority on coaching comments on the requirements of future leaders in this way: "leaders for the future need to have values and vision and to be authentic and agile, aligned and on purpose. Add awareness and responsibility to the mix, self-belief, and a good measure of emotional intelligence, and we have a powerful recipe. All these ingredients are organic, home grown, and carbon neutral for nothing is imported, in fact, they are already just where you are and waiting to be harvested."

I submit that the optimum Executive Leadership development depends on context and content. If you wish to successfully bring about culture change, increase your personal effectiveness and provide a greater return on investment in you, then you have to own and drive your self-knowledge and personal development, aligned to the corporate vision and values, and driven by meaningful goals. One-on-one executive coaching provides a safe space for senior leaders to reflect, learn, and develop in a non-judgemental environment within a trust-based relationship. Focused Executive Leadership coaching, as part of a thoughtful and holistic set of development initiatives, delivered by skilled and purposeful executive coaches will give us the quality of future senior leaders we need.

WHAT IF I DON'T KNOW MYSELF?

Lacking in authenticity as an Executive Leader will inevitably mean that you will experience many repercussions. It will be difficult for you to build a genuine followership without clearly establishing alignment between your values and your actions in the eyes of others. Your leadership voice, by whatever medium you communicate, whether explicitly or implicitly, will either lend credence to your actions or damage your credibility *(Communicate Messages)*. It is hard to visibly live your values if you lack clarity about what they are. It is hard to always demonstrate your authentic best self if you have not put the effort in to know, understand and develop yourself.

As you will discover, it is hard for others to trust us if they do not perceive us as credible, and that is unlikely to happen quickly unless we specifically provide what others need to create this perception. Trust is a necessary precursor to influence, and without influence at the executive level it becomes very difficult to foster goodwill, build productive alliances *(Address Politics)* and bring about lasting change in an ethical, sustainable and reputation-enhancing way *(Build Trust)*.

In short, if you do not work hard to know yourself and demonstrate authentic leadership, your long-term success will be <u>*very*</u> much harder to build and sustain.

MODELS, TOOLS AND TECHNIQUES

To support my work in my executive coaching practice, I use a selection of coaching tools and models. Below, I introduce you to a few of these that you can use as thinking and reflection tools, and I will also discuss a couple that you can use with the aid of a qualified practitioner or coach to help build your self-awareness.

Know Yourself

REFLECTIVE JOURNALING

Reflective journaling is an excellent way to develop self-awareness. By writing and reflecting on your responses to experiences you can better understand your reactions and emotions, make meanings from experiences, draw conclusions and create transformational change. Applying the insights

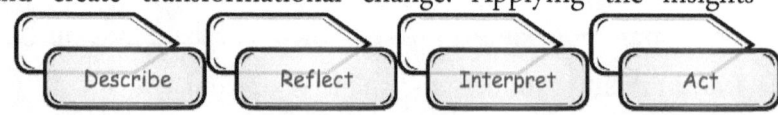

gained from critical reflection enables you to challenge your beliefs, try new things and construct action plans for increased effectiveness. Journaling, then, is a series of writings, much like conversations with yourself, which document your experiences in terms of a four-step process as follows:

- **Describe** - What took place? (describe the situation objectively, the facts – who, what where, when, how many, etc.)
- **Reflect** - How did you respond to what happened? (your physical sensations, emotional response, thoughts and your actions)
- **Interpret** - What have you learned? What conclusions or deeper meaning can you draw?
- **Act** - What you will do differently? What action will you take to apply your learning?

Your journal entries will provide you with the self-knowledge and self-awareness to figure out who you are, and what is working for you and why (so that you can repeat it).

You will also be able to identify what isn't working (so that you can avoid it) and what could work better (so you can do things differently, and increase your effectiveness).

SELF-REFLECTION ACTIVITY

Try this activity. Equip yourself eight sheets of lined paper, or mark up eight pages in Journal. On the top of each sheet or page write one of the following statements:

- I am...
- I can...
- I enjoy...
- I am proud of...
- I have difficulty...
- I would like to...
- I am good at...
- I think of myself as...

Complete these statements twenty times each creating unique, authentic statements each time. It may take you several sessions and a few periods of quiet reflection to consider and write them all. Then look at each statement objectively and critically. Ask yourself:

- What have I learned about myself?
- What, if anything would I like to be different?
- What do the results of this activity say about me?
- Are there any thoughts or beliefs that I wish to challenge?

Write down any new beliefs, thoughts or actions that you think would be useful in your Journal and note any

Know Yourself

development needs in your Development Planner.

JOHARI WINDOW

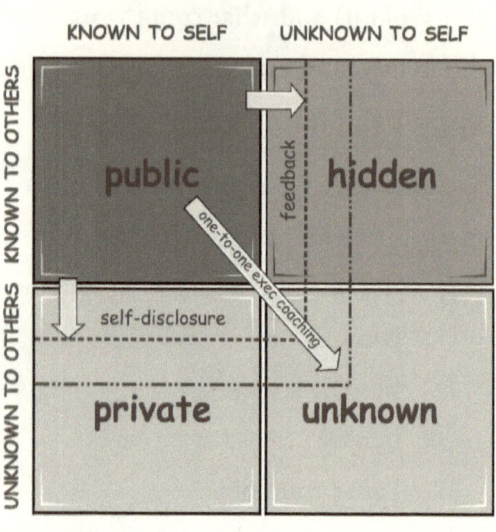

The Johari window was created by Joseph Luft and Harry Ingham in 1955. This simple and useful psychological tool can be used for personal development and for building self-awareness. By thinking through the quadrants or by working through the quadrants with your coach you will better understand the dynamics of your significant relationships. By sharing more about yourself with others you can build trust and create the environment where others feel safe to open up to you.

By opening yourself up to feedback from others, you will make inroads into the area that is 'Hidden' from yourself by better understanding how you are perceived by them and what actions may be causing issues between you. By working with a coach you will become aware of what is going on for you at a deeper level, and you will be able to use that information to inform your development.

LOGICAL LEVELS MODELS

The Logical Levels model was developed by Robert Dilts, based

```
        Purpose
       Identity
    Values and Beliefs
   Skills and Capabilities
  Attitudes and Behaviors
       Environment
```

on the work of Gregory Bateson. This model (also known as the logical levels of change) is very useful for helping to understand or effect change from an individual, team, organisation or societal point of view. Change made at one level will affect all the levels below. Thus, it is helpful when you are 'stuck' in a problem at one level (or trying to gain awareness of what is happening for you at that level, and why), to refocus on what is happening at the level above.

THE LOGICAL LEVELS MODEL

A coach will work with the coachee to help to reframe issues to unlock the possibilities for change and action, first working through the levels to understand how they perceive the current situation at every level. They will then work through the model to enable their coachee to describe their future desired state at each level, i.e. 'the best that I can be.'

POINTS OF INTEREST

Know Yourself

Some of the key facets of this chapter include:

- **The importance of knowing yourself:** When you dig deep to identify and appropriately utilize all the resources you have within, you operate consciously and with focus, driven by a clear purpose that evokes passion in self and others. With the demonstration of authentic leadership you become a respected, trusted leader, worthy of followership and credible in the eyes of those with whom trust-based relationships are vital for sustainable influence and long-term effectiveness. Authenticity creates a context within which you will be perceived by others, and your actions and behaviours assessed. *How well do you know yourself and how much clarity do you have about the purpose that drives you?*

- **Being an authentic leader:** Authentic leadership is demonstrated by those who are self-aware, and who willingly show their true selves to their followers; they do not see leadership as a performance to impress others. Rather, they recognize the need to be aware of who and what they are, and also what they are not. *How can you ensure that you demonstrate authentic leadership at all times?*

- **Building insight and self-knowledge:** Authentic Executive Leaders work hard to understand themselves and their emotions. They speak their values and beliefs rather than hide them. Through utilising a range of methods and approaches such as self-assessment, personal reflection and coaching, Executive Leaders can continue to develop their personal effectiveness and maximize the value of their contribution to their organisation. *How will you continue to build the insight and self-knowledge you need to share your values and beliefs and feelings to others?*

- **Continuing your personal growth:** Knowing yourself is an ongoing journey towards self-actualization. Just as Executive Leaders guide and develop their organisations so that they continue to stay relevant and thrive, so they must also develop themselves with the same focus, aligning their personal development with the needs of the organisation. *How will you ensure that you continue to develop and grow in order to remain relevant and effective in your role as an Executive Leader?*

Remember as you read through the chapter to reflect on the questions asked, note what comes up in your journal. Use the resources we have made available to you to check and assess where you are. Following reflection, witness what comes up for you and make a note of that and any actions required.

UNDERSTAND THE BUSINESS

Casey Kroll

"To lead a successful organisation one must be able to motivate, lead and engage individuals, groups and teams, often without direct interaction. There is no greater demotivation than to realize that a 'leader' does not understand what makes this particular organisation successful."
Casey Kroll

Understand The Business
WHY BOTHER?

Because we must! Leaders at every level of the organisation must understand not just what the organisation's business is, but how it works, and how to leverage its people, resources, structures, and processes – both at the micro and macro levels. To do this, one needs to understand why it exists, its environments, values, passions, purpose and vision. By doing so, one can apply their personal and the organisational resources in such a way as to obtain the greatest benefits with the least effort.

This understanding must transcend the basics of the organisation's role, its culture, its resources, and its processes to include a thorough understanding of the specific actions and investments needed for success. Every organisation has actions or abilities that can greatly magnify the force and impact that the organisation exerts. Executive leaders must know which of these provide the greatest benefit with the lowest level of effort: what they are, how to use them and most importantly why, when and where to use them.

One often quoted but still relevant example of a lever to success is the package delivery company Federal Express. The founder knew, without a doubt, that their key to success was to 'absolutely positively' deliver packages overnight. He focused all of his efforts, drove the organisation's material investments, shaped its culture and staffed the organisation with people dedicated to that vision. He knew, without a doubt that customers would not be willing to pay three to 30 times the cost of alternate delivery methods that 'sometimes' or 'most of the time' get their package delivered.

Executive leaders cannot bring the many elements of executive leadership elegantly together, into an integrated whole, without understanding the organisation's business (what it is about) and its unique levers – both current and future. This understanding is essential and unique. All electronics companies do not share the same levers to success, nor do all service organisations, and nor do all governmental agencies.

For executive leaders, personally, and for the organisations that they help lead, the short list of the most powerful actions and investments is evolving and co-dependent on the evolving environment and internal resources. This very short list must be used to prioritize efforts, and to reduce the chances of an organisation wasting resources out of habit or established patterns. Lessons learned ten or even five years ago may no longer be valid, no matter how expensive they were to learn, nor how valuable they were at the time.

Too often I have read about, or personally experienced, a new senior executive coming into an organisation and in cookie-cutter like fashion applying 'solutions' that were learned or copied from elsewhere. Different size organisations with differing pools of human talent and culture can have different solutions to the same problem. Any actions taken, and the results that they achieve, in a $500 million size electronics company are probably not appropriate or even available to one of $50 million in size, even though they may compete in the

Understand The Business

same 'industry'. Conversely, to even attempt to have a larger organisation re-shape itself as fast as the one just 10% its size would be impossible, even laughable, in most circumstances. The understanding of levers goes beyond just the organisation's size; it includes the entire spectrum of the external and internal environments and context of the organisation.

Tropman and Wooten provide a holistic method of understanding the business in their paper "Executive Leadership: A 7C Approach." It introduces us to the concept of an organisation's contexts, both technical and social. The "Technical Context' of an organisation includes business processes, design capability, scientific technologies, etc. The 'Community' or social context includes its people, values, government environment, markets, etc. The combination of these contexts allows one to see the organisation through the eyes of its stakeholders - both as groups and as individuals. These include its customers or clients, those that support it / contribute to it, those with power over it, and most importantly, those negatively affected by it. An Executive Leader must understand and relate to both of these contexts in order to make good judgments, identify and evaluate alternatives, and understand impacts on the business as their

		Leadership (Community)	
		High	Low
Executiveship (Technical)	High	Statesperson	Specialist
	Low	Generalist	Loner

Navigate

contexts evolve.

Understand The Business

Tropman and Wooten characterize leadership styles by how well an executive leader relates to these contexts. They are not apparently judging but describing. In a small entrepreneurial organisation, such as an advertising agency, hair salon, or accounting firm, the specialist approach may be fully appropriate. In other situations, such as a large, governmental organisation, the generalist approach may be appropriate if the leader has brought others in to fill in the missing bits.

Jim Collins (in Good to Great) introduced the idea of an organisation's 'hedgehogs', which are those drivers of success that simultaneously meet three interrelated criteria:

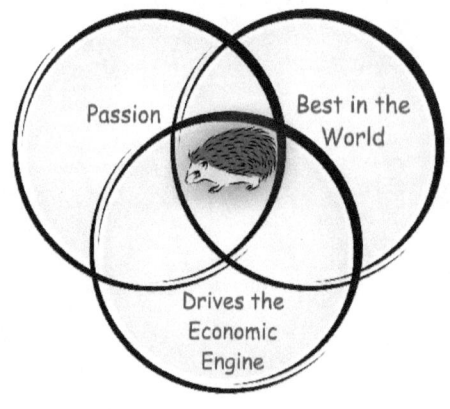

1. **What are they deeply passionate about?** Passion goes beyond merely wanting something. It amplifies the organisation's core values and culture.

2. **What are they the best at in the world?** Not just really good, but the best. If you cannot be the best in the world at your core business, it cannot be the basis for your hedgehog.

3. **What drives their economic engine?** Requires an understanding of the workings of the markets, operations, investment, people, etc. Reduce this to a simple form; for

example: "Profit per customer visit", "Profit per employee", "Customer satisfaction as indicated by voluntary return visits."

In many ways, my concept of an organisation's levers and Collins' hedgehogs are similar: they may not be obvious; they may take years to identify, and they drive the economic engine of the organisation, or of oneself.

Perhaps the biggest difference between these two concepts is that the organisational levers, in the context I am applying them, are by definition evolving and dynamic. Therefore, they require continued, close attention to the organisation's contexts in order to ensure their continuing relevance and effectiveness. Too many times, once highly successful organisations continue to apply outdated or outmoded hedgehogs, leaving themselves without relevance as the organisation's contexts shifted either slowly or cataclysmically.

A key attribute of organisations' levers is that they extend impact beyond the level of effort exerted. One needs to continually ask oneself 'For every unit of effort or resources expended, is this the single most beneficial way in which I can apply it?' If not, do not do it – find the one that is! Why would anyone in their right mind expend resources, in less than optimal ways? Just to 'cover all of the bases by accident' or 'just because we have always done it' or 'it takes too much thought and effort to understand what the best way is'.

These levers are hard to identify, partly due to the fact that they must be uniquely tailored to the organisation's contexts.

And, partly because their full effect may not be obvious unless they are applied as a coordinated whole. To have a transportation system between major metropolitan areas able to transport packages between cities overnight, without the local delivery mechanism as well, would be useless.

Organisational and personal levers cannot be copied and applied from others; they are unique to each and focused on delivering the strategic intent of that particular person or organisation. Although they may share commonalities with similar people or organisations at the same place in life, or in the same market or sector. They must be crafted and tailored in order to help you and your organisation fulfil its unique mission to its fullest potential.

HOW TO DO IT

Identifying these levers is not an easy, nor a quick, task. Doing so is dependent upon knowing the technical and social contexts of the organisation. This effort may transcend us personally and may only be successful by synthesizing the sensing, thoughts, experience, and assessments of others within the organisation. We must have the systems and personnel in place to assist us with this ongoing, dynamic process.

Our understanding of the business knows no bounds. We must:

- Understand its mission and role within the larger context
- Understand its stakeholders, its competitors, its technologies
- Understand it internally as it is today: its people,

resources, values and politics
- Continually build leaders within the organisation
- Expand our connections to aid the gathering of essential information and insights in order to understand the business
- Strike appropriate balances first in setting and then in implementing the strategy(ies)
- Manage performance, ours and our organisation's, by putting in place effective systems to measure performance, progress and results
- Take appropriate corrective actions. We expect this of sports teams, why not of ourselves and our organisations?

In smaller organisations, it is an entrepreneurial leader who has the combination of insights, understanding, and vision to make the organisation work – be it a small business or a focused local not-for-profit organisation. For the entrepreneur-led organisations, the challenge for the entrepreneur is to realize when and if to replace or supplement their personal assessment of organisational approaches with those of others that they have brought into the organisation.

In larger organisations, as Executive Leaders, it is our responsibility not just to identify and apply these levers in areas that we personally, directly influence. We must also establish the systems and processes to ensure that the entire organisation is aware of and focused on identifying and maximizing the appropriate levers.

Unless we are blessed with considerable insight and

Understand The Business

understanding we seldom see all of these levers upfront. Some are easier to identify than others; we and many others will see them easily. These are not the ones that help us be the best executive leader than we can be – they help us be the obvious leader, doing the obvious.

To help us identify the 'not so obvious ones,' we may need help. We can get this help by:

1. Giving voice to those within the organisation,
2. Encouraging conversations,
3. Building passion,
4. Identifying situations from which we and the organisation can experiment and learn,
5. Taking measured experiments, at appropriate levels of risk, some through thoughtful analysis up-front, and others more by accident through application of hindsight,
6. Building a better, more comprehensive understanding of the actions, resources, performance measures, and approaches to the business of the organisation.
7. From this understanding, focusing our mission, our vision, our strategies, our resources, performance management - all of the compass points - to achieve synergy and compounded effort.

One of the most misapplied levers that an executive leader has at their disposal is organisation structure. Too often organisations are structured as mimics of other organisations, frequently looking and acting just like the one the new CEO just left, even when that structure is not appropriate to the new organisation. At times, usually just after a new entrant to a sector shows early success, other new and restructuring organisations tend to copy the structures of the recent star. This frequently happens even when that structure may not be relevant to their unique contexts.

The single, most influential input to deciding the structure of the organisation ought to be the answer to the following question: *"How should we be structured so that our stakeholders (most importantly our customers or clients) receive the greatest value from us, through their own eyes?"*

Be wary of walking into a new situation with a pocket full of answers – you may be answering the wrong questions! Instead, walk in with a pocket full of questions; questions that help you gain understanding. It is very hard to un-break an egg.

Yes, do the obvious ones quickly. But take the time to ensure that the most significant decisions, the most important ones, are applied to areas that give the 'most bang for the buck'. And that they are tailored to the success of the organisation within both of its evolving contexts.

Grow your understanding of the business beyond that of a 'Mr. or Ms. Obvious'. Understand it well enough that you will be able to identify and apply the most powerful visions, investments, approaches, resources, and values that you can, enabling both you and your organisation to excel.

FOUNDATIONS FOR UNDERSTANDING THE BUSINESS

Understand The Business

In some ways, building a foundation is the easy, but potentially time-consuming bit. Alone or in conjunction with staff, executive leaders must gather and synthesize an understanding of the environment within which the organisation operates and of the organisation itself. This includes potential alternative, more lucrative places. When one gets to crafting strategies, we must not ask a damn good milk cow, no matter how well fed and trained and motivated, no matter how powerful the vision and the communication, to win a horse race. It will not get there from the barn within which it currently, rightfully resides. One should think instead of generating higher value results from the same cow, such as starting a boutique creamery with hand-crafted cheeses. Even at this simplistic level, a dairy farmer must understand their business well enough to be able to recognize an average old milk cow from one with gold ribbon award potential; else they will be using the wrong ones for brood stock! Alternatively, continuing our analogy, sell the cow and buy a damn good race horse if your goal, your mission, is to win a horse race. Without first understanding the business, most strategies will be doomed to failure as they are being written.

The first part of understanding the business is a solid understanding of the environment and markets within which the organisation operates. There are many tools to help with this process. One such approach is the identification of the Political, Economic, Social, and Technological (PEST) factors in the organisation's environment.

Another categorization is Environment, Political, Informatic, Social, Technological, Economic and Legal (EPISTEL) factors. A third one is STEER analysis: Socio-cultural, Technological, Economic, Ecological, and Regulatory factors. The important point here is to pick one that has an emphasis on, and insight into factors that have the biggest impact on the environment within which your organisation operates, or potentially could operate. Pick, build on it over time. Strive for not just data but understanding within the context.

The second part of the foundation is an understanding of yourself and your organisation. Self-understanding includes many dimensions, many of which are covered in various sections within this book. It also includes psychometric factors that we do not touch on.

In some regards, understanding our organisation is an easier task. Tools to guide us include McKinsey's classic '7 S' model:

- **Strategy** – The organisation's alignment of resources and capabilities to "win" in its market, the focus of our current discussions.
- **Structure** – How the organisation is organised. It includes roles, responsibilities and accountability relationships.
- **Systems** – The business and technical infrastructure that employees use on a day to day basis to accomplish their aims and goals.
- **Shared Values** – The set of traits, behaviours and characteristics that the organisation follows. This would

Understand The Business

include the organisation's mission and vision.
- **Style** – The behavioural elements the organisational leadership uses and culture of interaction.
- **Staff** – The employee base, staffing plans and talent management.
- **Skills** – The ability to do the organisation's work. It reflects in the performance of the organisation.

Many other tools that are available to help with this today are focused on and expand certain specific areas of this model. Others combine and redefine these concepts for specific markets or industry sectors, such as 'not-for-profits', government, healthcare etc.

Find one that suits your organisation's industry, not your organisation. Use it. Build on it. Drive for understanding. Remember – the results of any such assessment are dynamic. They change; the organisation continues to evolve. Stay in touch with where it is, where it is going, and how fast it is going there.

To assist you in gathering the underlying data, and then building an understanding of your organisation's external and internal factors, we have provided a spreadsheet template that has been specifically tailored to operating organisations and not-for-profits. It has come from the study and synthesis of the best portions of dozens of these tools. It has complete instructions and guidance for its use and application.

WHAT IF WE DON'T?

Without the identification and application of the levers to

success, everything that the organisation undertakes will only be accomplished by brute, plodding force. This non-leveraged approach consumes scarce resources, the most important ones being the talent and effort of the people within the organisation, and it consumes time, ever-marching time.

At the very least, wasting our personal and personnel resources on plodding approaches to an organisation's business quickly demotivates the best of these resources soonest. Thereby, turning one's best players into merely good ones, and the good ones into acceptable ones. As executive leaders, our focus must be on just the opposite. By establishing mission, visions, directions and goals, our investments and everything that we do can to help turn acceptable players into good ones and good players into great ones and let the great players lead. If you are lucky enough to have this within your organisation, you can soar unhindered but still focused by your clear vision.

Time is the only resource available to organisations that can never be restored nor replenished. Many refer to the fictitious activity of 'saving time' by altering their approach to tasks. If one could truly save time, it could be stored in a bottle, or on a shelf, or in an account somewhere, to be drawn upon when needed. We must make wise choices for ourselves personally, and for our organisations, so as to not waste time, and to use it more efficiently or effectively. As in many sports events, gaining possession of the ball, or having a turn at the bat, happens only a limited number of times within the game. A wasted turn cannot be replayed. Every turn must be used

Understand The Business

effectively. Our organisations face these same conditions. We, as executive leaders must minimize our and our organisations' wasted turns at bat.

Even more significantly, failure to understand the business of the organisation, will, as referenced above, relegate it to irrelevance.

Navigate
POINTS OF INTEREST

Some of the key facets of this chapter include:

- **Understanding technical context:** How well do you understand the "Technical Context' of your organisation and industry? This includes the business processes, design capability, scientific technologies, etc. that are the underlying enablers of value creation. If you do not, how can you gain this understanding?

- **Understanding social context:** The 'Community' or social context includes its people, values, government environment, markets, etc. As Executive Leaders, we must understand these and their impact, favourable or unfavourable, on us and our organisation. Do you? Do know how to gain this understanding if you do not possess it now?

- **Identifying what uniquely drives success:** If we do not know what is driving our success, we cannot invest to perpetuate it. What are the very few, often only one, critical issues that can take one or one's organisation from poor to good or from good to outstanding? If you do not know what these are, have you developed a methodology for discovering them, and updating them as circumstances evolve?

- **The need of knowing where one is really 'best in the world':** How can we be truly effective or efficient at what we do if we are not the best in the world at it? How can we motivate and lead with the goal of 'mediocrity'? How many sports coaches approach a season with the goal of finishing in last place? Have you heard someone justify their organisation's or department's performance with words like 'We are not as bad as some others.'? The bottom line is "Where do you and your organisation deserve the Executive Leadership Olympic gold medal?

- **Building passion for all of the above:** Building passion is easy. Building constructive passion can be very challenging. Do you know how to build passion – in yourself and others? Do you give voice to those around you personally, and also to those within the organisation you help lead? Do you encourage conversations at and between levels? Do you have well-formed and communicated vision, values and mission?

Remember as you read through the chapter to reflect on the questions asked, note what comes up in your journal. Use the resources we have made available to you to check and assess where you are. Following reflection, witness what comes up for you and make a note of that and any actions required.

CREATE VISION

Rahul Dogra

"Begin with the end in mind."
Stephen Covey

An organisation can spend considerable time shaping the strategic intent based on their current mission (where they are) and future aspirational vision (where they want to be). Moreover, it will ultimately impact its allocation of resources and investments. The same can be applied to the Executive Leader where the forming and acting upon their personal vision shapes their current and future activities and provides direction.

Most leadership discussion starts with crafting a personal vision statement, which in its simplest form provides a clear understanding of where you want to be and consider:

- How do you make your personal vision happen?
- Where are you now and where do you want to be?
- On what is your personal vision based? Myth or reality?
- Is your personal vision aligned to who you are, your values and leadership style?
- In what time frame is your vision based?

I have met many leaders who have taken time out to consider and create their personal vision statement. However, as soon as they return to reality, they forget their short, snappy statement, and there is no longer alignment with their declared actions. They may even place it on a card on the desk but despite staring at it every day, they see through it as if it no longer exists.

A personal vision is powerful when we live it, and there is congruence between what you believe in and what you actually do.

When John F. Kennedy declared that the U.S.A. wanted to put a man on the moon, this was not some random statement based on spin and dreams. Many of the components required to make this happen were already in place, the vision became the catalyst to turn it into reality.

As an Executive Leader, your personal vision will impact the team and other stakeholders. It should be important to you, but equally consider how it will shape the beliefs, behaviours, direction and actions of others.

Your personal vision should have alignment with the organisation's strategic vision. Achieving your personal success is highly dependent on the organisation achieving its success, and there should be a mutually symbiotic relationship that results in win-win outcomes.

WHAT IS A PERSONAL VISION?

It is a declaration of where you want to be at some point in the future. It belongs to you and sounds easy to do, but for some takes years of trial and error to discover. For others, they have a very clear image of what they want to achieve both in their personal and working lives.

It encompasses your emotional aspirations, representing a view of the future – *your future*. The difficulty is that we do not have full control of the future. A vision can often creep from being something that is galvanising and motivational to an aspirational picture that is sketchy, and you have no idea of how to achieve it. Through your vision, you create a set of goals and objectives. The challenge is to identify how to convert it into reality.

I went to a mid-sized organisation that was successful and led by a leader who had lofty ambitions of turning his company into a market leader within a relatively short period. Despite all the success they had, and continued to have, it was simply not possible to dislodge the large multi-nationals that had had a majority hold over the market. The ambition of the leader was admirable, but he never communicated how to achieve it. There was no explanation of what actions and activities were needed to create success. The result was that none of the senior management team believed that the vision was possible, and they did not back their leader.

WARNING: Do not lock yourself in a room and brainstorm a personal vision statement that is short and snappy unless you are prepared to:

- Understand how to achieve it
- Live it
- Communicate it
- Gauge success and failure by it

Otherwise, the vision statement will remain short and snappy and eventually become meaningless to you. In Stephen Covey's book "The *7 Habits of Highly Effective People*". The second habit is "begin with the end in mind" that provides a focus on where you want to be and becomes a guiding principle for your daily work and personal life.

The corporate world is awash with strategic vision and mission statements, guiding the organisation's activities. When developed and delivered successfully, they allow an organisation to fulfil its strategic intent. An analysis of this process, can be used to develop and deliver your personal leadership vision.

The strategic planning and analysis process aims to fulfil the organisational mission (where it is now and why it exists) and the vision (where it wants to be). It becomes the driver to create cascading operational objectives, goals and activities. However, is the starting point the vision itself? Do we just get together in a room and create it? Prior to forming the vision, assess the values of the organisation, what it stands for, its principles and heritage. These will shape the organisation, its culture, resources, processes, leadership and management style.

When I work with an organisation, I often find that some employees understand its values, but many do not. So, if the values are not understood and embraced by all, then how can it fulfil its strategic mandate, if everyone is not operating in the same direction?

You cannot create a personal vision in isolation without considering all of the following five factors from a holistic and collective perspective:

1. **Values** - Identify what you stand for and believe. In essence, your life is built on these pillars (both personal and career). They form the bedrock foundations that ultimately shape your mission and vision.
2. **Mission** – Where are you now? It represents a benchmark of your life and career, your leadership style and approach, and a reflection of your capabilities, strengths, weaknesses

and areas of continual development.

3. **Vision** - A consideration of your future articulated through a statement, and the timeframes involved in achieving this. Remember that this is yours and should not be shaped by others. Consider what *you* want to achieve and aspire to.

4. **Critical success factors** - If you know where you want to get to, consider then how you will get there. These represent actions taken on a continual basis that combine to enable you to achieve your personal vision. They may include: life-long learning, developing and enhancing your critical thinking skills and improving your interpersonal communications skills. It is important to identify and select the crucial factors that will enable you to achieve your personal vision.

5. **Your personal vision scorecard** - A measurement tool that allows you to continually assess and measures how you are moving towards your vision, and provides a basis for measuring success and progress.

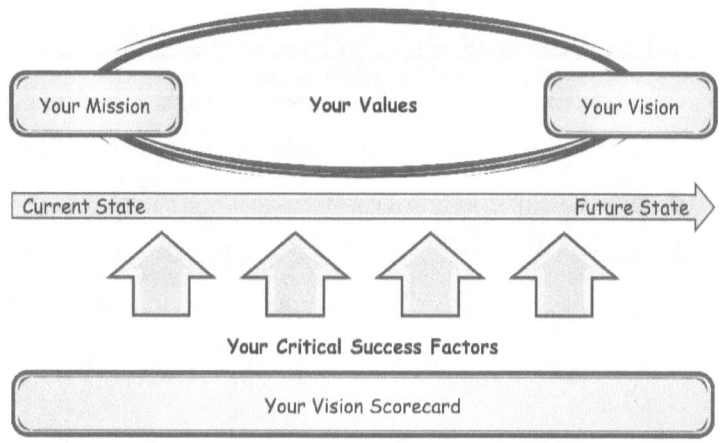

Navigate
CRITICAL SUCCESS FACTORS

A clear picture of your personal vision allows you to understand your core values and allows you internalise what you believe in and what you are not prepared to change or sacrifice. It helps shape your decision-making process and ascertain to what extent it fits in with the needs of the organisation. It will direct you and form your leadership approach in both the short and long term.

View your vision as a passport. It is transportable and transferable, can be used in existing and future roles, creating choices and guiding opportunities for you. After establishing it, think how it will be translated into actions and ensure that it runs in parallel with your leadership style. Are your actions aligned to your vision? Consider the implications of a point when there is no longer alignment between your personal vision and the organisation's strategic vision. Fundamentally you are operating against your values, creating a moral dilemma. I come across a number of leaders dissatisfied with their work environment. When you drill down, you discover that they are working against what they believe in (their values) and no longer enjoy the environment in which they operate.

I met one leader who worked in a fast, vibrant group that was going through change and was unhappy with his work. When I worked with him, it was clear that the values of the organisation were no longer going in the same direction as his. He had a choice: stay and be unhappy and compound that unhappiness, or leave and seek other opportunities. He decided to leave on his birthday, and the result was that his career got back on track, and all future decisions benchmarked against his vision and values.

Your vision requires alignment with the organisation's strategic vision and should be jointly pointing in the same direction. If they are not, then are you being authentic? It will become apparent sooner rather than later that you are unable to deliver if the alignment is not there. The organisational vision should be reflective of what you aspire to.

Your vision is personal to you and should act as a motivator on a daily basis. The vision if not enacted upon is pointless, so periodically reflecting on whether you are moving towards it is useful. If it needs to be adapted or changed, then do not be afraid and be decisive, else you will continue to operate against what feels right. The ability to adapt forms the basis of good leadership behaviours.

HOW DO I CREATE MY VISION AND ENABLE IT?

It represents a journey that you will travel. It sets a clear path and creating it is dependent on a complete understanding of your aspirations and goals. Identify your values, and where you are currently, in relation to your vision. Once identified, it needs to be communicated to others so that they understand your direction. Measuring that progress through a vision scorecard assesses where you are and where you need to be. This journey takes the following series of steps:

Navigate

STEP ONE - ARTICULATE YOUR VALUES.

- Articulate your values
- Identify your mission
- Formulate your vision
- Communicate and enable your vision
- Measure progress

If you take a look at an onion and cut it in half, you see a series of concentric layers, each tightly packed around each other. The outside layer represents your vision, the direction that you want to take. It is what others around you will see and experience when they come into contact with you. At the core are your values that shape your vision.

Values are those beliefs and factors that shape everything you do both in and outside of the work environment. These help you to identify **what to do, what not to do** and **what to stop doing**. They represent the guiding elements through which you can benchmark success and failure.

They may include: being passionate, respectful of others, having freedom to make choices, focusing on your family, being comfortable, having courage, continually learning, inspiring others, being innovative, focusing on others, your faith, aspiring for greater goals, etc.

Having identified the list of your values, now go back and rank them by considering what are the most and least important. You may even take this opportunity to whittle the list down. Ranking values can be difficult to do and requires a fair degree of self-reflection, and most importantly, honesty. These are your values, and they drive you and shape your authentic leadership approach (*Know Yourself*).

On the whole, your values remain fairly stable and will not change tremendously, unless there are significant changes in your life. As your goals and aspirations change, you need to benchmark these against your values. Building on your understanding of your values and developing a fuller, more comprehensive insight of you as an individual, provides a holistic appreciation of your drivers, abilities and competencies. Ingles (1994) identifies a framework known as the Extraordinarily Realistic Self-Image (ERSI), providing an overall picture of one's self and undertaken by evaluating a number of critical components:

- Investigating your work and critically reflecting on your role
- Reflecting: investigating the alignment of your personal and professional goals now and in the future
- Gaining objective feedback from others, including trusted colleagues, family and associates
- Making sense of the range of self-assessment metrics that you have undoubtedly taken over the years. What do they mean and how can / do you use this information?

An executive coach can aid and assist, providing an impartial, overview of the data and its implications

- Investigating the congruence between your personal needs and the organisational requirements and consider if there is alignment

STEP TWO - IDENTIFY YOUR MISSION STATEMENT.

Your mission statement provides a benchmark of where you are now, what your purpose is and how you go about achieving success. If you have followed step one, then you will find the creation of your mission statement relatively easy to do, since you have undertaken a fair degree of critical self-assessment and evaluation of who you are and what you represent.

To assist further, think about your value add. What do you uniquely offer your organisation, the factors that make a difference? What is your leadership value add? Is it the ability to be holistic, making decisions, industry knowledge?

After developing a clear appreciation of where you are, you can now increase clarity over where you are going.

STEP THREE - FORMULATE YOUR VISION STATEMENT.

Reflecting on steps one and two, consider the big picture and think about where you want to be. Prior to creating a vision statement, consider:

- What do you want to achieve, where are you going, and what are your next challenges? Now benchmark this against your values and ensure alignment

- If you were to look at yourself and your career in the future, what would you have achieved and what would you represent? It may help to write a quick phrase to describe this point in time, to help visualise your vision (e.g., "become the master chef")
- How does your vision fit with the organisation you currently work with and the direction in which it is progressing?
- Are your aspirations clear and unambiguous? Can you communicate this to others? Can you use this to drive the organisation forwards and get employees and other stakeholders on board?
- Does your vision challenge you? Is it something that will transcend a statement and allow you to utilise it on a continual basis?

Success is not created by having a vision alone; it requires a series of foundational factors (critical success factors). These have to be maintained and nurtured to deliver the vision. If you look at a successful consulting firm, its accomplishments are based on a number of factors. They include recruiting and nurturing the best talent, investing in continual learning programs, identifying internal talent, building client relationships, delivering value add to the customer. Once these factors are identified the organisation continually invests and protects them as they are the key to continuous growth and provide a differential in terms of competitiveness.

Navigate

If you have a clear idea of where you are going, then you must identify and continue to feed and nurture your critical success factors. These are your strategic pillars. They will be different for each and every one of us, but may include:

- Continuous life-long learning, including coaching and mentoring
- Investing in one's health
- Seeking and developing life-long relationships at all levels
- Leveraging lessons learned
- Creating win-win strategies both internally and externally to the organisation

Having reflected on these critical success factors, craft and develop your vision statement by addressing the following:

1. Bullet-point your values and then rank them
2. Draw a picture or create a metaphor that reflects your personal vision
3. What are your critical success factors that enable the vision?
4. Do not attempt to write a vision statement yet, but capture some words and phrases that reflect your vision
5. Now using all of the above, create your personal vision statement. It can be a sentence or a small paragraph

Having written your vision, be prepared to revisit it initially in one, three and six months to ensure that it remains valid. Also, periodically re-assessing it helps to maintain and keep it alive.

STEP FOUR - COMMUNICATE AND ENABLE YOUR VISION.

Spending a considerable amount of time developing, but not communicating your vision becomes self-defeating. You cannot lead if you do not have followers, and followers will join your journey if your vision is communicated to all stakeholders (*Communicate Messages*).

- Your message has to be consistent, and you need to ensure that others internalise your message. It may take time, but it is an investment in others that allows your personal vision to come to fruition through the combined activities of all
- Evaluate the other points on the Executive Leadership compass to assess how they can be leveraged to assist you

You will set the tone and pace of progress, and there will barriers in the way, but you must steer through these to achieve success.

STEP FIVE - MEASURE PROGRESS.

The energy created around the development of your personal vision can quickly dissipate away if there is no momentum. It is provided by measuring progress towards the vision (remember that this is a continuous journey you are on). Components may include managing change and creating an innovative environment. These factors you have selected will require careful and systematic monitoring to ensure progress in the right direction. For each factor consider a set of qualitative and quantitative measurement elements identifying:

- **Objectives** – What are the goals that are to be achieved and over what time frame?
- **Measures** – What parameters will you focus on to measure progress?
- **Targets** – What are they and are they realistic?
- **Initiatives** – What actions will be undertaken to achieve progress towards the goals?

These measures should also be periodically reviewed to identify where you are and what progress is being made to achieve your personal vision. A template for use in tracking your steps to Create Vision is available at

https://daledarley.com/my-executive-leadership/.

WHAT IF I DO NOT HAVE A VISION?

You can function and operate as a leader without it, but look at the implications from a number of perspectives. Firstly, consider yours. Without your vision, are you able to identify your long-term aspirations? Where are you going, or will incremental progression suffice?

Now look it at from the perspective of those you lead. A team is a group of individuals with a common goal. Your personal vision provides long-term direction, perspective and leadership. Finally, view it from the perspective of the organisation. How can you deliver the strategic intent without a clear image of your vision and knowledge of what to do and crucially *what not to do*?

POINTS OF INTEREST

Some of the key facets of this chapter include:

- **Developing your personal vision:** Your personal vision is yours but equally it shapes the beliefs, behaviours, direction, and actions of others. Does your vision enable you to understand your core values? Does your vision shape your decision-making process? Has your vision been communicated to other stakeholders?

- **Linking your vision with the organisation:** Is your personal vision aligned with the organisation's vision? Is there any disconnect and what are the implications for you?

Remember as you read through the chapter to reflect on the questions asked, note what comes up in your journal. Use the resources we have made available to you to check and assess where you are. Following reflection, witness what comes up for you and make a note of that and any actions required.

STRIKE BALANCES

Dale Darley

"Life is a matter of balance. There is no past or future just a pivot point in between."

"Life is like riding a bicycle. To keep your balance you must keep moving"
Albert Einstein

Strike Balances

When I think of balance I see a picture of a tightrope walker making his or her way across the canyon, with just their inner quiet, belief and focus. Every step they take, they move closer to firm foundations, one false move and they fall out of control into the vastness and inevitable death.

In organisations, everything is a balancing act. The very act of closing an order requires a balance between the ethics of getting the order and delivering the goods, presupposing you can deliver what you say you can. A balance, then, between what the customer is willing to pay and what you perceive as the value of the goods. Other balances you need to strike are: the invoice and payment, the order for raw materials and cash in the bank to pay for them or the availability of people to make the products.

Consider the potential investment in new plant and machinery to get longer-term returns, versus the short-term pressures and diversion of resources from other activities. We understand the tasks involved and the processes we must follow to make the organisation tick, but when do we focus on the relationship between each of the transactions to ensure that there is a balance?

- What about work-life balance or how do you balance the desire to go higher in your organisation with the needs of a growing family?
- What about the need to strike a balance between your personal needs and an organisation in financial difficulty? Would you consider re-location, a pay freeze,

Navigate

take redundancy or change jobs?

Striking a balance is about taking part of each side of the equation in order to satisfy something else –the outcome you desire. Before you consider the outcome, you must also consider the bigger picture. What balances are required to make sure the big picture is delivered? It is in the nature of organisations (and in life) that striking a balance is a skill that with practice and experience becomes (somewhat) easier.

My roles have often been at the front end, crafting brands and winning business. The pressure on me to bring home the bacon was always enormous, and when I did, the rest of the business then took the focus of pressure, as they then had to deliver. In the early days of my career, what I noticed was often missing was the glue in the middle – the relationship where the two teams could strike the right balance to ensure timely ethical sales in at the front end and quality deliveries at the back end. If you have ever worked in software, you will understand how the drive to sell software that is often incomplete causes log jams at the back end. This is because systems and processes go out of the window as developers struggle to write code that needs to be delivered working and to customer expectations by a given date.

I cannot be alone in feeling frustrated with this attitude? It was only when later, as an executive leader, I was able to become the pivot, a kind of central point, with 360 vision between my team, the rest of the organisation and customers.

WHAT IS BALANCE?

Strike Balances

So what is balance then? Balance is a range of things equally distributed. - the tightrope walker, the rope, balancing pole and the focus. In other words, the goal we are striving for and the factors that shape the journey; where all factors become inputs into delivering the result – namely the goal. It is a relationship that is struck between all of these things. It is about when and where to put your attention. Which part of the balancing act needs your attention and which is the priority at any given time. Striking balances requires constant feedback from all of its factors, where communication, perspective and being in tune with conditions around them are essential.

If the tightrope walker does not communicate, maintain a perspective, have their senses finely tuned (think wind and temperature and rope tension) and create an agreement with all parts of the equation, how would he or she keep their balance and reach their destination? Those key skills and the relationship between all aspects are what keep the balance and enable our tightrope walker to reach their goal – the other side. It is, I am sure you will agree, a delicately calibrated dynamic process.

Executive leaders are pivot points in the equation. They are a pivot because they set direction, make decisions, define the strategy and set direction on the allocation of resources. The executive leadership team has the responsibility to consider all aspects of the business, holistically and consider how to strike balances between task, process, resources, relationships, communication, strategy, vision, passion and purpose. Not to mention brand, performance, innovation, cash flow... Striking balances is another imperative, too much of a good thing is a bad thing – most people will die if they breathe 100% oxygen!

A balanced approach to executive leadership and organisational development acknowledges every person and organisation are different and at different places in its lifecycle, therefore, different approaches to strike balances are necessary. In addition, each organisation, just like a person, goes through a developmental process. At all of these stages, different philosophies and styles will be appropriate. In *Plan Journeys*, we are asked to think about how planning forces the rigor of the process whilst making it appear that actions are spontaneous as you navigate the different personal and organisational variables and life stages. That is, strike a balance, do the hard work and make it look effortless. If the plan is not in place, striking balances will never be achieved.

Consider the things that might need balancing in your organisation, the balance sheet might look something like this:

- Profit and corporate social responsibility
- Incremental or transformation change
- Short-term results or long-term commitment
- Process or creativity
- Manage or lead
- Empowerment or control
- Centralised versus distributed power
- Local or global

- Intuition or action
- Risk taking or risk avoiding
- Work or life
- Train or buy in expertise / direct labour or contractors
- Complexity or simplicity

Which of the 16 compass points are vital for you to strike balances?

Which end of each equation is the right one? Which factors provide the answer? The answer is, it depends on the situation and the long and short term factors and forces surrounding you and the business. What we do not want is to be constantly running from one extreme to another.

The Executive Leader is the fulcrum, who, with sometimes delicate precision balances all of the parts to create an equal equation. This is a key leadership function. They create the right leverage to support the business and allocate its resources effectively. According to what is needed, the Executive Leader places him/herself at the right point to ensure an equal measure of input and output forces.

WHY DO WE NEED BALANCE?

We balance so that we can set the pace and prioritise the needs of the business. It is not about how fast we can run the race, but what shape we are in when we cross the finish line. The questions we need to be asking are, 'when do we need to speed up?' and 'where?'. And when do we slow down and when? Finally, when do we put on cruise control and breathe? Just as in sailboat racing, speed may not matter at all – it may be the route one takes around the course, or the ability to execute changes in direction flawlessly that win the race and of course (with luck) a favourable wind.

Whilst all areas of business are important, and none should be neglected, it is about ensuring we do not exhaust our organisational heart. We know that every system is composed of interrelated components and what we want is to optimise the performance of each, relative to the goals of your organisation. By neglecting or only focusing on one area, the others become unstable. Imagine if you neglected to invoice your customers, you would soon be out of business without cash coming in.

Allied to that is concentrating on short term thinking: looking at quarterly or annual reviews and quick fixes. When this happens long term thinking gets lost in the chaos of short-termism. It is imperative that instead of focusing on one part of your organisation and deeming its isolated efficiency gains as success, your organisation must connect all of the pieces to create a unified success. Those pieces include all of the inner organisational imperatives along with the external forces.

Consider an organisation like Virgin, who must balance profit with people and the planet. They have an enormous task. In an interview with Neil Duffy (Chairman and Founder of Tribe Management for Real Leaders), Branson says *"Doing good is good for business. Whether you're an emerging entrepreneur or a champion of industry, now is an exciting time to explore the next great frontier where business puts people, planet and profit at its core. With the constraints of the world's resources, business as usual won't work: we need to build new business models."*

You need balance so that your organisation continues to operate at its highest level so that it satisfies its stakeholders. All of your stakeholders will have expectations, which need to be identified and added to the alchemic mix. Those expectations might include external factors such as the environment and internal elements required by law, like diversity.

Where change is the only constant, constant change requires a balanced approached and balanced people, not only for the sanity of the people but the sustainability of your organisation. Remember even those people whom you consider to be challenging are helping you to strike a balance. The challengers make you think; they question the system and in creating this 'confusion' or 'chaos' you are being given a great gift (yes really!) – a chance to see another's perspective. Those 'odd balls' and especially naysayers may be an advantage, even a necessity! They help us strike balances – they help us avoid the sins of 'group think.' This concept can appear to fly in the face of creating visions, etc., but an organisation must know where and how severely to draw the line on 'following the program.' All of Collins' 'GREAT' companies that failed had significant amounts of loving themselves too much and not being willing to listen to the voices that pointed out the problems with the approaches being followed.

When the leader shares and communicates change via the interconnectedness of values, vision and mission to create a unified identity, it provides a strong pull, which in an empowered culture creates shared ownership.

Each organisation's balance point will be different because of the nature of the business and the forces that surround it. It is not just that we want to be mediocre and in the middle, we may need to balance innovation and growth with bought in expertise and creating a global footprint.

All too often organisations create confusion when attempting to create innovation. You only have to think about the mobile phone market, what happened to the phone that just makes calls? Sometimes simple is best and to achieve simplicity we need that 360-degree holistic view and to listen.

Because the Executive Leader is the fulcrum, a lever that helps to create balance and the one who can exert the power to change things, they play an integral part in the balancing act that is the day to day business and long term strategy.

For the Executive Leader, their balance is a contributory factor to the healthy balance sheet of the organisation. In the chapter *Lead Strategies,* Casey says *"Our understanding of the business knows no bounds. We must understand its mission and role within the larger context; we must understand its stakeholders, its competitors, its technologies and we must understand it internally: its people, resources, values and politics."*

That is a big responsibility and as Executive Leaders it is paramount that our goals include staying balanced and grounded. A healthy business needs a healthy leader and just as an organisation can become exhausted and worn out with wavering vision and inaction, so can you. By staying grounded and taking that 360 holistic view you can remain balanced, disrupt the chaos (and use its learning wisely), bringing calm and focus, so that you can complete what needs to be done now, with an eye on the longer term.

THE STRUGGLE FOR POWER AND BALANCE

You have I am sure been challenged with making decisions and working collaboratively. Think back to a time when you knew you couldn't fail, what was your default pattern of behaviour? Did you exercise positional power or personal power? Did the collaboration turn into a competition? What happened whilst you were busy competing with your colleagues? Did the competition win the business?

Position power is the authority you get from your position or role. Personal power is the authority you command, based on who you are. You only have to look out into the world of the celebrity to see how both their positional and personal power influences others.

It is time to consider how to use your position wisely. Of course with position comes power in the form of authority, but it does not give you the power to lead. People are following you because they want to. Then consider your personal power and how you collaborate with others.

Balancing positional power and personal power is a challenge. Your goal must be to strike a balance between using authority and being collaborative so that the strategy can be implemented, and people enjoy implementing it.

You can and will get resistance; any concerns with your decisions need to be addressed by engaging with people and seeing resistance as feedback. A tough call, I know. Conflict is an opportunity for change. By demonstrating respect, you will build trust (*Build Trust*). Trust is another imperative in sharing power and striking balances.

HOW

Just how do you get to the other side? Walk the tightrope, juggle the spinning plates and stay focused on delivering a unified wholesome organisation, which satisfies all stakeholders and enables you to stay grounded?

The Executive Leader needs to: -

- Be a hero, inspire and help create and nurture other heroes
- Understand your organisation (*Understand The Business*) and the context in which it operates
- Take a holistic view
- Create a balance sheet
- Refer to the plan. Live, breathe and adapt where necessary

HEROES

You, the Executive Leader, have to be a hero, a champion amongst your peers, where you use the compass at the heart of what you do and who you are. Use the compass to guide your heart to connect to and engage with the hearts of other people.

Strike Balances

When you do, you will motivate others to want to walk beside you, not behind or in front. Side-by-side empowered, trusted teams collaborating for the highest good where their personal brand and personal power are connected to your organisation's brand, creating a common purpose, common identity and balance.

Can this utopia be achieved? Possibly.

I am a fan of champions at all levels. If we have an executive leadership team which come together without egos to be the heart and soul of the organisation and work to keep the beat and energy vibrating at the same frequency. Who together have a clear idea of how they can support the organisations overarching vision, who can communicate values, mission, passion and purpose to their people, and engage them in creating and executing strategies and tactics, then yes.

STRIKE YOUR BALANCES BY:

- Setting goals without compromising relationships with people (Sometimes goals are set that can be perceived as being compromising, but they may need communicating too to understand the big picture and to get people on-board)
- Trusting people and providing autonomy whilst still keeping an overseeing eye
- Confront difficult situations and deal with conflict by considering everyone's view in the context of the conflict
- Being professional and having the ability to have friendships with colleagues, remember you do not need

Navigate

to be friends to have a professional relationship

- Walking a mile in another man's shoes. Treat others how they want to be treated (if you can work that out) and treat as you would want to be treated

Strike Balances

UNDERSTANDING YOUR ORGANISATION AND THE CONTEXT IN WHICH IT OPERATES.

Connect values, vision and mission to strategy and communicate it: Vision and strategy need to be cascaded down and integrated at all levels. You will, of course, have heard this countless times. You will also have heard many say that overall organisational vision is usually crafted at the top and often stays there.

Some come to work just to do their jobs and get their take home pay. Not everyone will care about the vision, or know what the strategy is; sadly organisations and people often operate in vacuums. You cannot change the world, but you can find like-minded people, other heroes who will help you to strike a balance between those who understand and do, and those who want to only perform at a lower level in your organisation.

Now let's imagine that your organisation is a system: work out how the system works, try things, theorise, take action, feedback, and utilise that new knowledge to create a more efficient system. Understand that every system has variations. Never underestimate the power of people to misunderstand and misinterpret the same instruction – it is the nature of the beast.

To strike a balance the Executive Leader must: -

- Work out how the system works and challenge it, so that it can be optimised
- Break it into smaller chunks, to understand how the

'chunks' work and then fit them back into the whole, so that they operate more efficiently and effectively
- Look for cross-cutting themes and then put them back into silos
- Disrupt the process and flow and then undo the confusion by reconnecting and sequencing the parts
- Constantly scan what's going on inside your organisation and what is happening in the wider world

TAKING A 360 DEGREE

From different vantage points: If you climbed to the highest mountain and looked down and around you, the view of your organisation and your place in it would be very different to the view you get standing at the bottom looking up and wondering how. As you climb higher or move to another place, the view will change. Using tools and methodologies which allow you to view the business from different vantage points with different eyes will indeed bring about a new perspective. Striking balances also, very importantly, includes knowing when the only acceptable balance point is 'all or nothing.' I.E. 'failure is not option', and 'this is the path and destination – if you do not agree, get off the boat or get thrown off.' Great leaders know when 'it must be' and know when variation can be allowed or even encouraged. Many of Churchill's greatest speeches were about 100% commitment and 100% doing what it takes.

STRIKE YOUR BALANCES BY:
- Going to the top and looking down

- Being at the bottom looking up, thus enabling you to understand the challenges and requirements to tie the top to the bottom
- Looking forwards and backwards
- Stepping in another stakeholder's shoes

BALANCE THE COMPASS EXERCISE

Do this balancing the compass exercise to give yourself an overall perspective of where you are. The exercise can be found at

https://daledarley.com/my-executive-leadership/

THE BUSINESS BALANCE SHEET EXERCISE

In this exercise, you and your team make a list of what you believe needs balancing and then work together to brainstorm how you balance things that seem to oppose each other. The exercise can be found at

https://daledarley.com/my-executive-leadership/

When you have done the exercise, remember that balance is something that can be achieved regardless of lifecycle phase with the right people. It requires a commitment to try and consider the potentially conflicting area in a positive manner. By adjusting the weighting (reference the plan here) or the balancing point, balance will be maintained. When a change in direction or deviation from the plan is required, weigh it up against your balance sheet and test it, assess the risks, consider different scenarios with different variables; when you see where the wobble points are, you will know where and how to strike balances.

REFER TO THE PLAN

In Plan Journeys Casey says, "It is most likely that we are simultaneously pursuing multi-dimensional journeys crossing and intertwining many segments of our being – our personal journeys, journeys with family and friends, professional journeys and the journeys where we lead our organisations." In the quest to strike a balance, ask 'is the plan (more likely multiple plans) taking you in the right direction',' is it the right plan', 'have you stuck to the plan', 'if not why not, if yes, why?' Always refer to the plan, reflect and amend as necessary in light of what is emerging, not too often otherwise you will end up going in circles. Take the plans and strike balances in accordance with them. The decisions will not always be easy; we understand that, use the compass and the knowledge you gain from this voyage of discovery to strike the right balance at this point given the context and situation.

WHAT IF YOU DIDN'T STRIKE BALANCES?

Balanced forces will either push or pull in equal measure and without balance there is chaos, exhaustion and corrosion. Like the tight rope walker, we fall, and more significantly, we take many others with us, some of them innocent of any wrong-doing! Without collaboration, strong teams and individuals dedicated to a common goal you cannot and will not have a balance. If you do not plan and take action, then you will never be able to strike balances. And like the tightrope walker, it takes practice and building a sixth sense of understanding the many

Strike Balances

factors that come to play in making our decisions.

Navigate
POINTS OF INTEREST

Some of the key facets of this chapter include:

- Do you know how to strike balances for yourself? Your family? Your organisation? Do you have a process to ensure the quality of your efforts in doing this?
- Do you revisit the balances regularly and make adjustments?
- Where do you need to focus your attention in striking balances for you personally?
- Where do you need to focus your attention in striking balances for your organisation?

Remember as you read through the chapter to reflect on questions asked, note what comes up in your journal. Use the resources we have made available to you to check and assess where you are. Following reflection, witness what comes up for you and make a note of that and any actions required.

LEAD STRATEGIES

Casey Kroll

*"Did you ever observe to whom the accidents (of discovery) happen?
Chance favours only the prepared mind."*
Louis Pasteur

Lead Strategies

Planning, at any level, whether for us personally or for our organisation, cannot be effective nor efficient without an overarching strategy or interrelated portfolio of strategies that are relevant to the circumstances at hand. I have been part of and have overheard even more numerous discussions on 'what are the differences between strategy and planning', often with each side not even listening to the alternate point of view. To simplify our discussions here, we shall adapt specific definitions of each and then apply them consistently throughout this book. Strategy is setting the short- and long-term goals, and then choosing the major methods for achieving them. Thereby, enabling ourselves and / or our organisation to at least survive, if not thrive, today and definitely to thrive in the future. Planning as was covered in our opening chapter includes more than just setting a route to our goal or destination. It includes identifying the necessary actions, determining the necessary resources, and estimating the costs and the timing of our actions.

At the organisational level, there are as many views on what strategy is as there are on how to develop strategies. The key to success of an organisation is, without a doubt, the appropriateness of its strategy to its situation. And for those in, or seeking, Executive Leadership roles the prime duty must be to develop and execute effective strategies for the organisation or their portion of it.

Our individual role in the development and implementation of strategy may vary widely based on our particular role and our level within the organisation. In an increasingly dynamic world, with ever more limited resources, how well we do this, at all levels, is essential to the future of the organisation.

We do not need to do all of the required research, development and planning by ourselves. In smaller organisations or for us personally this may be the case. But in larger organisations it is our responsibility to ensure that effective strategies are developed and implemented. We must lead the way, set the tone and ensure results.

The sad truth of the matter is that even for once great organisations, many strategies fail, in spite of the dedication of vast resources. For example, the Eastman Kodak Company, who once dominated the consumer photography marketplace for more than fifty years, had fallen into bankruptcy and liquidation. Most of its assets were sold off due to repeated failures in addressing digital technology in its market. This is especially saddening when one realizes that Kodak invented digital photography, had vastly more relevant patents than any competitor and had successfully led the application of this technology in medical imaging! This sad fact gives us new insight into the phrase 'Pretty as a picture!' We must ensure that our organisation does not become a Kodak!

There have been many studies of what makes organisations excel, only to have many of those noted soon fall from grace. For *Good to Great*, Jim Collins and his team researched thousands of companies. They analysed their performance over many years and researched many aspects of how the companies were run and structured. Their goal was to identify not just good, but great companies. Within three years of the economic collapse of 2008, only two of the eleven companies had managed to significantly beat the Dow Jones Industrial Average, and three were essentially tied with it. Three went bankrupt, one had been bought out, and one survived only because of a government-funded bailout. Hardly 'great' performance, is it? What can we learn from these sad but true stories whose plots are perpetually repeated with new actors every decade? One possible answer is that it is not easy to succeed in the long haul. We can be 'good' for a while, but it is necessary for us to truly understand if our success is due to true greatness or if it is due to many short-term lucky coincidences. Another potential lesson is 'We must stick to it' – finding and implementing those strategies necessary to keep us and our organisations relevant and healthy.

Leading strategies, therefore, must be our prime Executive Leadership role for it is strategies that set the direction enabling us personally, and our organisation, to survive / thrive today and to thrive in the future. Think of strategy development as the orchestra leader of the compass points, drawing from them, feeding them and coordinating the others into an integrated whole. To thrive today and merely survive in the future is clear evidence that we have left our self or our organisation weaker in our wake. This highlights a challenging dilemma – striking the balance of results today versus results tomorrow. This dilemma is greater and greater as executive leaders are often under increasing pressure for short-term results. To not just succeed but to thrive as individuals and as executive leaders we must bring our full kit of the approaches – all 16 compass points – to bear.

In this chapter, we will explore these concepts and insights further, and provide you with coaching, tools and techniques to help address this pivotal role.

WHAT IS STRATEGY?

As stated above, 'strategy' involves settings the short- and long-term goals then choosing the major methods for achieving them. This enables ourselves and / or our organisation to at least survive if not thrive today and definitely to thrive in the future. It includes the clear determination of the mission, the setting of specific goals to be accomplished and the high-level approaches to be taken in fulfilling the mission and accomplishing the goals. This must be done whilst simultaneously creating advantages that will make attainment of further goals easier. 'Planning' includes developing the specific actions, costs, resources, timing and communications needed to achieve these goals.

The GPS analogy is that the strategy says where we are going, why we are going there and the basics of how we will get there. Each of these elements is an essential part of the strategy. For example one of our multiple personal 'missions' may be to establish a jointly-owned family vacation property with the specific goals of fostering a healthy work-life balance.

Additionally, it would nurture multi-generational interaction, provide cost-effective holidays, and encourage the development of our 'extended family', in a location having low cost, convenient transportation. Obviously, this strategy would not work for all; family culture, personal interests, trust, as well as economic and geographic realities would all impact its suitability. The broader lesson from this simple example is that personal and organisational strategies must be suited to the internal and external realities of the situation.

Planning, then, ensures the development of the coordinated, specific actions to be taken to ensure successful attainment of the strategic intent.

"You've got to think about big things while you're doing small things, so that all the small things go in the right direction."

Alvin Toffler (author)

Strategy defines that destination and key way-points along the journey. It is around these that we build visions, craft our brands, communicate messages and cultivate passions. To do any of these without first establishing a realistic strategic goal, one that is based on understanding the circumstance and surroundings would be foolhardy at best. To do this well, we must understand the business of the organisation, often with the aid of the connections that we have fostered. In order to implement our strategy and its associated vision, we must be able to communicate where we are going, why we are going there, and how we intend to get there. Then, along the way, we must foster innovation, manage politics, build trust and facilitate change - all of the remaining compass points - to facilitate our own and our organisation's success.

Throughout this entire process, we must manage ourselves: knowing ourselves, developing ourselves, and crafting ourselves. We need to grow and evolve as circumstances, and our personal desires and dreams warrant. This is a dynamic, on-going process. One that we must do in a way that not just maintains, but fosters our authenticity and credibility else we, and our chosen goals, paths and approaches will not be credible. To do this well requires a personal strategy, around which we build our personal vision, plans and brand.

I have often been asked 'what is the most important aspect of implementing strategies'? The same answers apply personally and organisationally. The answers are easy; however, doing them, especially the third step is the quite difficult bit:

1. Knowing where to go and what to do in the future
2. Knowing where not to go and what not to do in the future
3. Knowing what to stop doing that you are doing now, in order to free resources and to focus on doing the essential bits for where you are going.

The first two are important, the third is essential. Failing to prune efforts, thereby squandering key resources on non-essential initiatives, deprives an organisation of its ability to adequately focus on and feed its future. If all initiatives are the highest priority, they are also the lowest priority. Failure to selectively prune leads to bloated, underperforming organisations. Very close linkage with the *Understand the Business* chapter is essential to getting this right

Reading about knitting is the easy bit, as is watching someone else do it; doing it, and sticking to it is the hard part. We all get better at most things with practice, even a failure if we do not learn from it! We all get better at most things when we have or build the right tools.

Let's now proceed with getting and building the right tools to enable us to build and lead strategies for ourselves and our organisation. Simultaneously, let's stop distracting ourselves from the important bits with habits and busy work that do not help us achieve our long-term goals.

WHY BOTHER?

As we have seen for other points, we bother because we must. To not bother to have a meaningful strategy is to have a strategy, albeit a very poor one. As Executive Leaders, we are accountable for our sins of omission. I know of no organisation today that claims to have excess resources for its tasks at hand. This may be due to learned helplessness, to ineffective use of the resources at hand or to the unwillingness / inability to get the right resources.

Technologies are rapidly evolving and riskier. I do not know if you ever done this, but I just completed a two-week-long exercise in recovering my personal computer from a very malicious virus. Only with the aid of Microsoft, Dell and many, many hours of my own time am I back to 80% of where I was two weeks prior. Are we, our organisations and our people ready to take advantage of and to simultaneously protect themselves from today's rapidly evolving and expanding technologies? Do we have backup and recovery plans or are we forging high-risk paths with our eyes closed to many pitfalls and challenges?

Recently, a very sudden, short-duration but massive and intense storm came through the area where I live. It struck a swath more than 200 miles wide in the midst of one the worst heat waves on record.

Flooding and uprooted trees were everywhere, disrupting electric power, sometimes requiring 10 days or more to restore it. This had a massive impact on basic necessities like drinking water, air conditioning and refrigeration.

Hospitals emergency generators exhausted their standby fuel supply, but more fuel could not be readily obtained because there was no electricity to power the gasoline pumps.

Cell phones could not operate because they could not be recharged and because of similar impact on the cell tower switching gear and on the internet which they rely on.

Food spoiled due to lack of refrigeration. Stores closed for many of these reasons and remained closed for others. Once the power started to come back on, many could still not do business. Without internet connections, the online Point-of-Sale and inventory systems could not process transactions and, even for those that could operate 'off-line', many clerks could not make change without the aid of electronic cash registers.

The lesson here is that we need strategies for not just where and how we are going, but for how to deal with the inevitable issues that will come up along the way. These issues could be due to 'unforeseen' circumstances, many of which should have been foreseen with better preparation and personal networks.

Throw into this mix the evolving nature of both our family, customers and our staff members. Their needs and perceptions are always evolving, but on occasion shifting suddenly and drastically. These sudden shifts in attitudes, needs, wants, and values may be a simple compression of a gradual, long-term drift. Or they may be a sharp change or even reversal, triggered by singular sudden unexpected events. An organisation's staff members of the millennial generation, as many pundits reflect, do not take dedication to their careers and places of employment as strongly as did previous generations. This could become a major impediment to western organisations competing in the global arena, and hence the need for sound strategies to ensure their future.

Even as a middle manager leading our respective section of a larger, more complex organisation, we can and must create *pockets of excellence.* We, the four authors, are talking to, and about, Executive Leadership in this book, not executive followers. Executive Leadership does not start once one has attained a position of Executive Leadership. It is grown, fostered and nurtured in preparation for being in such a position. I do not know you, but I suspect you are similar to me, in that I prefer my doctors to have the training and expertise to treat me before they practice medicine, not afterwards.

As mid-level leaders, set your strategies in support of the strategies of the larger organisation. Gain insights and understanding of the business. Build and foster your connections and your vision. Hone your skills and your brand. Build yourself. As an Executive Leader, your role is not just to discover yourself, it is to craft and to grow yourself in positive ways. Create your pocket of excellence, for yourself personally and those around you.

Why bother? We lead strategies because it is imperative that we do this. Failed strategies lead to failed initiatives, which in turn lead to failed visions, failed change management, failed brands, wasted resources and broken trust. We have dug ourselves, those around us, and our organisations a deeper, steeper hole to climb out of, with fewer resources at our disposal. This is not a good idea!

HOW TO LEAD STRATEGIES

Louis Pasteur got it right when he said 'chance favours the prepared mind.' This is especially true in today's world. For most of us, for both ourselves and for our organisation, we cannot clearly see 10, 5 or even 3 years in the future to make 'cast in stone' plans and commitments. What we MUST do is to have on-going processes of data gathering, collection and analysis in place so that we can lay out rational short, intermediate and longer-term waypoints. We must understand our own and our organisation's business well enough to predict the continuing evolution of our personal and the organisation's

Lead Strategies

decisions.

As with our GPS analogy, we must include sufficient flexibility in the how, the where and the when, to allow for and to circumvent unexpected traffic hazards. This may even mean refining or changing our ultimate destination. We must continually build and rebuild our personal and organisational human capabilities to be ready for the emerging needs.

For ourselves personally, and for our organisations, one of the most significant challenges is knowing when and how much to release elements of the past. This allows us to firmly grasp new methods, skills, attitudes and approaches of the future. This is not easy. Because of the significant, demonstrated success of their historic approaches, many Executive Leaders have tenaciously held onto the past as the world evolved past them. Many others too quickly or ineffectively chased one or more fads whilst consuming vast resources and time. Striking balances is not easy.

Great strategies come from the marriage and application of understanding and insight. Neither of these comes cheap. There are many models for helping leaders and managers to build understanding. In all of these, we must start  with an understanding of the business we are in, both for our organisation, and for ourselves. Additionally, we must understand people: ourselves and our constituencies: our family, our fellow employees, our clients, our investors/funders, etc. We must understand their capabilities, how to read them, how to lead them, and when to follow them.

As I shared earlier in this chapter, we do not need to do all of the required research, development and planning by ourselves. In smaller organisations or for ourselves personally, this may be the case. But in larger organisations it is our responsibility to ensure that effective strategies are developed and implemented. We must lead the way, set the tone and ensure results.

It is not uncommon to have more than one strategy as an organisation may serve multiple geographic markets, have multiple segments of current and

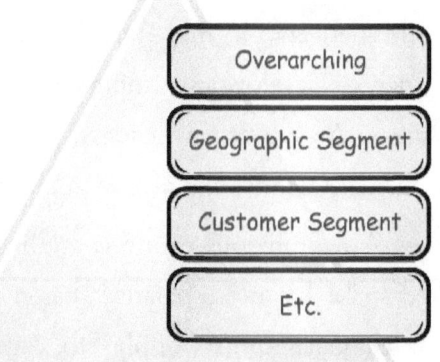

potential customers, or apply multiple key technologies. For ourselves, we may need multiple strategies corresponding to the many facets of our lives – family, faith, community, health, etc. It is only rational to craft an overarching strategy for the organisation or us as a whole, and then build independent or intertwined subsidiary strategies for key segments. One may need supportive IT, operations and succession management strategies as enablers of the overarching and subsidiary strategies.

Your role as an executive leader is to ensure that such a framework exists, and / or that your piece of the puzzle has its appropriate strategies in place.

BUILDING THE STRATEGY

Now comes the hard bit: taking these understandings and from them, as so-called raw materials, developing a strategy that maximizes our short-, intermediate- and longer-term objectives. Again, depending upon the size and complexity of the organisation, this may be the task of only a few at the top. Alternatively, it may be a process put in place to gather, analyse, develop and implement strategies at many levels and areas. As Executive Leaders, we need to get this done - by ourselves or through and with others.

A few obvious cautions are in order here. One is the need to strike balances. Balances based on wisdom. Our emotional intelligence must apply to ourselves, our view of the organisation and to the individuals within it. We do not do the organisation, nor its members, any favours by providing them with false senses about themselves; senses of capability, accomplishments or suitability. As I told you above, this was the tough bit.

As with our building of understanding of the environments and the organisation, there are numerous, almost too many, tools to help guide us.

Porter while studying the relative success of various markets developed his concept of the five forces that drive the rivalry within an industry. These forces, as he sees them, are threats of new entrants, threats of substitution, the relative amount and extent of customer power, the relative amount and extent of supplier power, and the degree of entrenched competition.

Another tool, mostly misapplied, is the structured analysis of Strengths, Weaknesses, Opportunities and Threats, called SWOT. In reality, it should be called TOWS as we must first understand our Threats and Opportunities before we can adequately categorize our capabilities as either Weaknesses or Strengths. Take, for example, someone who is 6'3" tall. This is often cited as an advantage by some. Obviously, they have never tried to cram a body this tall into most cars or aeroplane seats lately. On the other hand, most of us would see this as an advantage when reaching for the cereal boxes or sweets on the top shelf of the pantry.

A very powerful tool if applied diligently is the identification and focus on Core Competencies. Core competencies are more than mere strengths. They are capabilities that can provide us a clear strategic advantage in the future. If the competition can identify and build them

Lead Strategies

easily, they are not a core competency.

Here is a simple five-point test of core competencies:

1. **They are not easy to identify**, else everyone will do so, and will then start the potentially long process of building them. Better the competition does not see them until it is too late for them to adjust.

2. **They are difficult for competitors to replicate**, else they will do so. Look for your unique capabilities that build stakeholder value. These are potential core competencies.

3. **They can take years to develop**, both for us and anyone else. Getting a head start can be a long-term advantage.

4. **They add considerable value to our stakeholders**, now and in the future. If they are not adding value to our stakeholders, they cannot be the basis for competitive advantage. So what if we are good at something – it has to be a key, decision-driving value-adder for our stakeholders.

5. **They are aligned with our mission**. Back to our milk cow example. Having the best dairy barn in the county does not help us win a horse race unless we just plan to use the proceeds of our dairy business to buy a racehorse.

Things we do or have, that meet these criteria, are the areas we can use to build our future success upon. Feed them and nurture them as the most important investments that you can make. They are the keys to your future or your organisation.

"Every advantage is temporary."
Katerina Stoykova Klemer (poet)

By investing the time and effort to identify areas that add substantial unique stakeholder value, which are aligned with our mission, difficult and time-consuming for the competition to replicate, we can establish core competencies – i.e. competencies that are at the core of our ability to succeed. These we must build, feed and replenish because others are simultaneously working their own strategies in attempts to relegate us to second place or lower.

EXAMPLE STRATEGIES

Porter, along with his 5 Forces, has identified three 'winning strategies' to help guide our strategy development process. Essentially, his strategies can be summarized as 1) be the low-cost provider, 2) differentiate to increase the value or, 3) focus on narrow markets or applications where one can specialize.

Other tools which we will not cover, but which can be useful to you, include the BCG market share versus growth rate model and the GE /McKinsey Matrix model (Business Fit versus Market Attractiveness).

Each of these models, like others, have their place. That place depends upon where one is within an organisation, the level of maturity and capability the organisation possesses, the stakeholder needs and wants, and the business sector within which it participates.

To assist you in your development of strategies. I will summarize some specific examples that can be generalized across business sectors, at many levels of an organisation where successful strategies have been built in the past.

Lead Strategies

1. **Identify the 'unquestionable assumptions' of business models** or approaches to adding value for your stakeholders, and then question them. Of course, no one would pay $12.00 to have a package absolutely, positively delivered overnight, when they could use the US postal service and get in delivered three or four days for $0.45. Hence the birth of Federal Express (FedEx).

2. **Develop new, more powerful, or lower cost methods of delivering goods and services.** Do not assume that customers must visit a store to browse books. Or that orders may take weeks to fulfil. Or that consumers are happy paying a premium higher cost for immediate access due to the expenses associated with carrying high volumes of inventory that only occasionally sells. Hence the birth of Amazon.com.

3. **Find the exceptions and make them the rule.** Has your organisation ever, due to exceptional interest from the executive suite or due to 'one time' emergency events or special circumstances, operated in a very different manner? Sometimes accomplishing things in minutes that would normally take hours, or in hours those that would take days, or in days those that normally take weeks? Great! Now you have proved it can be done – make it happen routinely and effortlessly! When the Japanese-based automotive companies invaded the United States in the 1970s and 1980s, they effortlessly brought high levels of customer service and comfort throughout the buying and ownership process.

Things that the once 'Big Three' could only do under extreme duress.

4. **Reduce costs by providing only what is really required.** Do not waste resources on low-priority extras. For many segments of the population, getting from point A to point B was the only essential thing. They did not worry about perks, and building points for future travel. They infrequently travelled or were solely focused on cost. Hence the success of Southwest Airlines and other 'value, no-frills' airlines.

Can you find direct analogies to these organisational strategies in your personal life? Are there unique approaches that you can adopt to increase the value you add to yourself and your 'stakeholder', like your family and your friends? If we never ask ourselves these questions, we will never answer them. Ask them of yourself *NOW*!

IMPLEMENTING STRATEGY

This takes work. This takes resources. This can take time. Often we have limited time and limited resources. Therefore, we must make our strategic implementations effective and efficient. Build visions and use them, make connections and use them, build leaders and use them, communicate messages, manage change and performance, etc. In short use the other 15 compass points to get it done.

> "The essence of strategy is choosing what not to do."
> — Michael E. Porter (University Professor and Author)

Lead Strategies

Focus on where you and your organisation need to go. All other initiatives must be off limits. And most importantly, we must identify all of those other things that we are doing now that are diluting our ability to really do what we need to do, and then stop doing them. Stop distracting ourselves from the important initiatives.

WHAT REALLY HAPPENS

Seldom does a strategy or strategies create results exactly as anticipated. There are too many challenges to understanding and predicting the future. And, too many challenges in assessing and crafting effective organisations. Seldom is the future what we expected. This does not mean we should not develop strategies. It is even more proof that we must. We must have an understanding of our environments and our organisation. We must be familiar with analysing and assessing them. And we must be practiced at choosing courses of action and implementing them.

A powerful tool to help understand the implications of the dynamic nature of our future is to employ scenario or sensitivity analysis. These involve working through a range of both interrelated and unrelated changes in the assessment of the current and future events and conditions, in both our and the organisation's environment. Variables can include but are not limited to, economic performance, competitive actions, governmental policies, the capability of resources, unsuspected technology developments, voter preferences and changing values. Strive for an understanding of the implications of these variations, and take this variation into consideration as you develop your specific path forward. Evaluation criteria in selecting your path can include, amongst others, the amount of potential benefits, the cost or effort to get there, and relative risk or uncertainty.

When, not if, unanticipated events occur, we have a ready understanding of evolving situations and of the resources we can redeploy in alternate ways. We have better, more dynamic resources and systems in place. We have established and honed our ability to build visions, implement change, communicate, etc. We are ready for the future and adapt to it in dynamic ways. We build understandings, set plans, implement, then adjust and modify as an on-going process.

> *"Can you define 'plan' as 'a loose sequence of manifestly inadequate observations and conjectures, held together by panic, indecision, and ignorance'?*
>
> *If so, it was a very good plan."*
>
> Jonathan Stroud, The Ring of Solomon (author)

This is not meant to say 'embrace adhocracy.' This is not to say, just go through the motions, and if you do not succeed, just change your goals and move on. This is not to say you must have a 'no blame' culture where no one gets blamed for anything, and there is no standard for performance. There is usually a lot of blame to go around, starting with failures of leadership and diminishing from there on down.

It is to say, be ready for variation and be ready to adapt to it. Every time you take a failed path you have consumed resources, damaged your brands and impacted trust. Instead, adjust, modify and move on. The better your preparation, the smaller the adjustments you will have to make.

Remember Alvin Toffler's advice above about the small things. Our strategies do not have to be in exactly, precisely the right direction. However, the evolution of them needs to cluster around a series of evolving targets, thereby maximizing our results through synergy, as opposed to consuming them with 180-degree shifts in direction.

WHAT IF I DON'T?

Would you and your organisation enjoy being heralded as the next Kodak? Or as an example of a failed not-for-profit agency that has had to close its doors because it lost relevance with its clientele? Or as an example of a government agency that is bloated with bureaucracy and out of touch with the needs of its constituency? Or an example of someone who had 'great promise' versus one who 'accomplished so much with so little'. Is your answer 'No'? Good! Then get on with creating your personal pocket of excellence at whatever level you can. Use the experience gained to develop and hone your skills at leading strategy!

POINTS OF INTEREST

Some of the key facets of this chapter include:
- Crafting a process for strategy development
    - Do you understand strategic planning concepts well enough to apply them?

- In the particular circumstances faced today, should the process be top down, bottom up or some synergistic combination of these?
- What is the right level of associate or subordinate involvement with the challenges of understanding the environments, with the challenges of understanding true competencies, with identifying and developing core competencies?

- Who is best equipped to identify those special cases that could / should be converted to the norm in order to turn associates, stakeholders and customers into fans? If someone else did identify them, would you believe them?
- Who is best equipped to lay the plans for implementing the strategies?

  - **Applying the thoughts and concepts on organisational strategies to your personal life:** How can you use them to define and then maximize your attainment of the missions and goals you establish for yourself?
  - **Understanding the mission and role in context:** Do you have a clear understanding of this, for you personally and for your organisation? Have you communicated it well to others?
  - **Understanding the environments:** How complete is your personal and professional tool kit for doing this? Is it relevant to the circumstances at hand? Can you apply it? Do you see data or information or trends or more questions or answers?

Lead Strategies

- **Learning what to do, what not to do and what to stop doing:** The first two are important, the third is essential. Do you know where to feed and where to cut? Are you up to that task? Do you see that it gets done?

- **Implementing and adjusting to changing environments:** Do you have the right implementation and monitoring systems in place? Do you use them regularly? Are they effective? Do you show stubbornness or perseverance in the face of challenges or changing circumstances?

Remember as you read through the chapter to reflect on the questions asked, note what comes up in your journal. Use the resources we have made available to you to check and assess where you are. Following reflection, witness what comes up for you and make a note of that and any actions required.

MAKE CONNECTIONS

Rahul Dogra

"Invisible threads are the strongest ties "
Friedrich Nietzche

Make Connections

At the start of a career, the value-add an employee offers is based on their formal education and exposure to the working world. As an individual gains more experience and their career progresses, the focus moves away from their primary technical knowledge to another set of skills, colloquially known as soft skills. They include the ability to manage and then lead, motivate others, deal with performance issues, negotiate and influence stakeholders, gain buy-in to new initiatives and manage change, to name a few.

Those that become successful learn that there is a shift in gear from developing and refining their soft skills to an increased emphasis on who they know, and the ability to build and develop connections with others. These collectively become a network that is actively leveraged at the individual and group-wide levels. These relationships include:

- Internally, above and below the solid line (direct) and dotted line (indirect) reporting
- Externally, with key stakeholders such as customers, suppliers and shareholders

In one global organisation I have worked with, all new employees are told that successfully progressing their career is directly related to their ability to become successful networkers. What do they mean by this? It is not simply a case of increasing the number of entries in the address book. It requires a strategic approach. The goal of forming connections and creating a meaningful network is to form an extensive web of formal and informal relationships that creates value for all. This value-add has to be identified and can include a variety of factors such as:

- Knowledge transfer
- Mutual decision-making
- Influencing others to gain buy-in into new ideas
- Marketing the activities of the organisation both internally and externally
- Managing and delivering organisational change

Operating successfully involves shifting the focus away from the quantity to its *quality*. The aim being to form relationships with others to create mutual win-win benefits. Forming successful connections can, if used strategically, lead to success, defined by quality relationships shaped by high degrees of trust (*Build Trust*). It is qualitative in nature and if undertaken well allows an Executive Leader to deliver their results.

In this chapter, the focus is on the role of the Executive Leader in creating connections that provide access to a wider pool of knowledge and identify new opportunities to pursue. Success is increasingly defined by not what we know but whom we know. There is a focus on the quality of these connections, and the efforts required to maintain them, shaped by attention on connecting for mutual benefit.

WHAT IS MAKING CONNECTIONS?

When an individual enters an organisation and progresses through it, they have to focus on different qualities, depending on their role. Successful individuals that progress within an organisation will encounter the *what*, *how* and *who* model.

Make Connections

What *you know.* The credibility and value add of new employees with little working experience is based initially on their technical capabilities.

How *you are going about doing it.* As an individual's career progresses, more responsibilities are taken on, and roles increased with a steady shift in focus away from what an individual knows to how they go about doing their work. A new set of behavioural competencies need developing and enhancing. It becomes apparent, when moving into management positions, that skills include managing others, dealing with conflict and delivering change.

Who *you know.* When given greater responsibilities, the individual's locus of interest widens, involving more stakeholders that may be direct (vertical and horizontal) and indirect with dotted line responsibilities. In order to get results, the focus is not only on how they go about doing their tasks, but whom they know in terms of getting things done. There is now increased focus on getting activities delivered through the actions of others, including teams and other resource providers. These connections all need to be made and nurtured over time, and the focus is on creating a network of connections, defined by quality and its effectiveness.

Meeting someone and exchanging business cards is gathering contact details, not connecting. Those new to networking will furiously hand out business cards at events and leverage every social networking opportunity that presents itself, and they soon realise that they have a full and exhaustive network. However, what purpose does it serve?

Proactive and thoughtful networkers will know why they need to connect and create or select an opportunity where the purpose is clear. The strategic aim is to create connections that allow knowledge exchange to occur and leverage the opportunities presented. A contact becomes a connection when both parties gain mutual value add, and a win-win situation created, forming the basis of a meaningful relationship.

If there is a suitable investment in the relationship and it is reciprocal, it will build trust and improve communications, and becomes the line of least resistance towards building and maintaining long term relationships. We do not create success on our own and have to make connections in order to establish partnerships that are effective and mutually beneficial.

Success is defined by creating bi-directional value add. Each party will probably appreciate different things. The focus is on trying to be clear as to what you want from it and what the other individual wants. Identify the mutual overlap; the win-win or what is in it for us. Focusing on creating value add and working as a partnership, leads to stronger relationships, allowing greater collaboration and higher degrees of mutual trust.

WHY DO YOU NEED TO MAKE CONNECTIONS?

Having a network provides the Executive Leader access to a wider source of knowledge, information and data than exists within the environment the organisation operates in. It becomes useful when making decisions and reflecting on

Make Connections

strategic direction. It also provides an opportunity to meet other decision makers and influencers including customers. However, what about others that do not, at first glance, appear to be important? Perhaps a dotted line stakeholder that has no direct reporting responsibility could assist in securing resources or allow you to find out what is happening in other parts of the organisation.

Each connection consumes time, and if not managed, then the leader will suffer "network overload". A collection of extensive contacts that are not necessarily connections does not serve any real collective purpose. Be clear as to what purpose it will serve you *and* how you can serve them.

There are many reasons for building connections including:

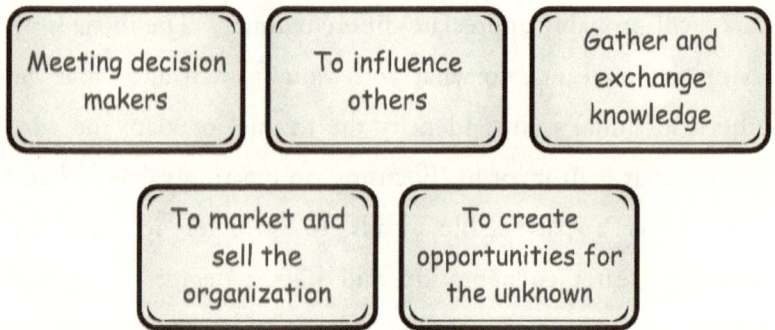

MEETING DECISION MAKERS

You will meet many decision makers that have various interests in terms of what you do, both formally and informally. Some of these decision makers will affect you currently; others may not today but could create mutually beneficial opportunities in the future. Investing in making connections with them can potentially create long-term dividends.

Of course, you cannot meet each and every decision maker but should take time to prioritize which relationships to form and which ones merit a face-to-face meeting and which warrant a virtual one. Once your series of connections starts to increase, you will be able to identify which decision makers you can get introductions to, via your existing network.

I met a marketing executive who went to an international sales conference. Their sole purpose was to meet others, put a name to a face and identify whom to network with for future activities. This initial investment was designed to pay long-term dividends.

TO INFLUENCE OTHERS

By creating connections, we have an opportunity to influence others for many activities such as implementing strategy and managing change.

Pink (2013) suggests that we spend a significant portion of our time influencing others. "People are now spending 40 percent of their time at work engaged in non-selling – persuading, influencing and convincing others that don't involve anyone making a purchase. We are devoting twenty-four minutes of every hour to moving others."

GATHER AND EXCHANGE KNOWLEDGE

As Executive Leaders, you need awareness of factors that shape the operating environment, and this knowledge exists both within and outside of the organisation. A smart approach is required to avoid knowledge overload. Consider what types of knowledge you need then rank them in terms of prioritisation.

Make Connections

Now identify which current connections can help and which need to be formed to assist in supporting your needs.

After establishing a network, the Executive Leader needs to adopt a mindset of knowledge trading involving supplying and seeking knowledge from your connections. If you only take but are not able to reciprocate, then the transactions are perceived as being one-directional, and the opportunities to leverage this network will become limited.

TO MARKET AND SELL THE ORGANISATION

Over the years, I have found that when conducting business with others, it is not between my organisation and theirs, but is in fact, between two individuals that happen to represent an organisation. It is personal and enables the greatest opportunity to present ideas, offer solutions and make others aware of what we are both currently and potentially undertaking.

TO CREATE OPPORTUNITIES FOR THE UNKNOWN

Creating success does not necessarily follow a linear process, and many opportunities arise just by being at the right place and right time. Being active with your network of connections, regularly exchanging knowledge, maintaining the relationship and seeking opportunities, builds an atmosphere of trust in which case potential opportunities may become visible.

HOW DO YOU MAKE CONNECTIONS?

Some central purpose has to drive the connections, and the network formed. A number of individual goals may shape it. The initial step is to identify them, by considering what is important to you currently and potentially in the future and consider the actions required to support it.

Once identified prioritise them and then *for each goal*, examine and assess:

- How well do your current connections support your goals? Write them down and then examine to see if the list is dominated only by a few. Are there other connections that you could enhance, but have not done so?
- What connections do you need to support your goals? If not developed, what do you need to do? Can an existing connection be leveraged to create an introduction?
- How can you reciprocate the value add to your connections, what can they get from you to strengthen the partnerships that exist?

MAPPING YOUR CONNECTIONS

For each of your goals, a map can be created to visualise the connections, as they exist, to assist you in identifying how your connection supports the goal. This process allows you to assess the effectiveness of the current valid state, and then consider what can be done to improve the quality of the network. There are many approaches to mapping, but I suggest the following approach:

- Identify the goal and then for it list out all the known stakeholders (anyone who has an interest in your activities) you have that allow you deliver it
- Having identified the stakeholders, focus on the

Make Connections

communications undertaken and consider: How do you currently communicate with your stakeholders? Is this face-to-face and in a formal or informal context, or is this conducted using email and social networks? What medium would be appropriate to improve the quality?

- Do not be afraid to analyse your list of stakeholders and assess who is important moving forwards and who is not. The primary goal should drive this; it should not become some arbitrary decision-making process. Undertaking the process enables the stakeholder list to remain current and focussed
- Who is missing from your stakeholder list? Who could assist your network and how do you go about acquiring additional members to join? Can you use your current list of contacts to acquire and expand it?
- A template for use in analysing your connections is available at https://daledarley.com/my-executive-leadership/.

CREATING WIN-WINS

The network will work to support your goals if you can offer something to your contacts. It is about creating their value add, developing reciprocity defined by mutual win-win mind-set. If the relationship becomes skewed in either direction such that it becomes win-lose or lose-win, then it loses its worth and becomes a burden on your time.

Maintaining the win-win situation means that you need to understand what you can offer others in exchange for their value add. Each contact will have different needs and wants, and the aim is to ascertain what they are and how you allocate sufficient time serving the contacts and the network in which you serve.

CREATING THE OPPORTUNITY AND TIME

Each and every interaction you make on a day to day basis is an opportunity to create a connection and forms part of any daily routine of a leader. In terms of creating a network and maintaining it, time is required to focus on what it is doing for you and what you are doing for it. Taking a proactive approach means taking time to engage actively with connections within your goal driven networks. What you get out of it will be driven by what you put into it, so ensure that you create the time to work it.

WHAT HAPPENS IF YOU DO NOT MAKE CONNECTIONS?

If time is not made to create connections and form a network, then the access to a wider pool of knowledge is made unavailable. This may limit your ability to understand what is happening and may happen in the future. It can impact your ability, and the organisation's, to effectively operate.

Making connections can appear to be a secondary activity, one that consumes time, which will be the case if there is no purpose and alignment between achieving your goals and creating long-term partnerships.

POINTS OF INTEREST

Make Connections

Some of the key facets of this chapter include:

- **Creating win-wins for each connection:** A successful connection is defined by creating bi-directional value add. Have you identified the bi-directional value-add for each connection? Do you have focus on not only what you want from the partnership but what the other individual wants?

- **Continual proactive influencing for authentic partnerships:** By creating connections, we have an opportunity to influence others. We need to influence others for many activities such as implementing strategy and managing change. Are you clear about what you are trying to influence? What goal are you seeking?

- **Knowledge sharing amongst your connections:** Once a network of connections has been established, the Executive Leader needs to adopt a mind-set of knowledge trading which involves supplying and seeking knowledge from your connections. Are you clear on what knowledge you are seeking? What knowledge are you trading with your connections?

Remember as you read through the chapter to reflect on the questions asked, note what comes up in your journal. Use the resources we have made available to you to check and assess where you are. Following reflection, witness what comes up for you and make a note of that and any actions required.

BUILD TRUST

Judi Williams

"You can't connect the dots looking forward; you can only connect them looking backwards. So you have to trust that the dots will somehow connect in your future. You have to trust in something - your gut, destiny, life, karma, whatever. This approach has never let me down, and it has made all the difference in my life"
Steve Jobs

Build Trust

What is trust? Is it a feeling? Is it 'real' or is it 'perceived'? How do we know when we have it, what it takes to acquire it, or that it is lost? Does it make us vulnerable or strong? Does it provide us with power, or render us powerless? These are the questions that we must answer for ourselves. We need to find the answers within ourselves before looking at the implications of trust (or the absence of) in the wider domain.

Trust is not a tangible thing in the practical sense of the word. Just like time, it is a concept that is vital to understand and manage if we are to be effective. When we look at the origins of the word, we will see many references to strength, fidelity, and confidence in its descriptors. It is apparent that the quality of the relationships that human beings have built, (originally with themselves, one another, and then subsequently with organisations and their brands) depends on trust.

Not surprisingly then, trust starts with trusting ourselves, trusting in ourselves, and understanding our own attitude towards trust. Are you a trusting person? Has your ability to offer trust been damaged by being let down in the past? Do you believe that your trust should be automatically offered, as we would expect others to trust us? Where do trust, openness and honesty figure in your personal values, and are your values demonstrated through your actions?

To operate at our best in any workplace, we must build relationships that address five different aspects of trust: -

- **Trust of integrity** which comes from the personal values that an individual's behaviour demonstrates

- **Trust of reputation** which is driven by what others in the network perceive
- **Trust of competence** which arises as a result of the knowledge and abilities that each has and shares with others
- **Trust of intention** which relies on the understanding that we each have each other's back
- **Trust of commitment** which is generated when we make and keep verbal contracts with each other

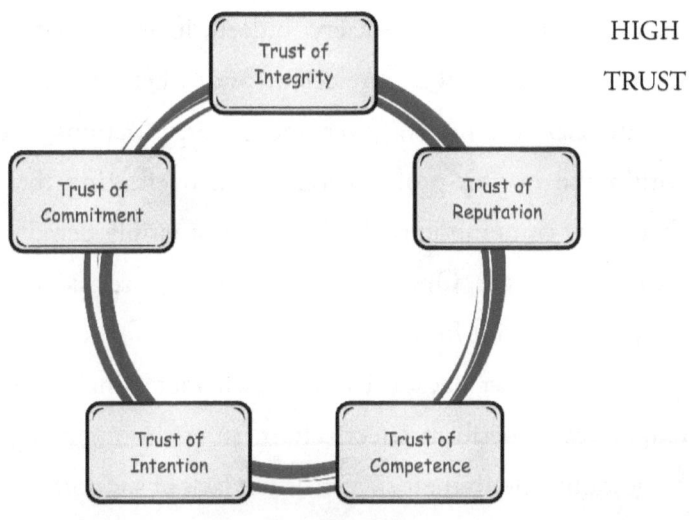

HIGH TRUST

RELATIONSHIPS

WHY SHOULD I BUILD TRUST?

"Society runs on trust." So says Bruce Schneier, in his excellent book 'Liars and Outliers'. Here he eloquently recounts the examples and research that support the view that trust is critical for order and for society to thrive. This also applies within the society that is an organisation, just as it would within personal and social relationships. He argues that trust is the foundation

upon which we build everything else. That it is the bedrock that is necessary for society to thrive.

As I sit writing this chapter, I am listening to the radio; it is a discussion about recent research that suggests that trust in organisations is at an all-time low. This is most likely partly a reflection of the trust in society where the interests of a significant minority are perceived to have significantly impacted the well-being of the majority.

This lack of trust does not appear to be limited to one sector, or one aspect of society; indeed, it prevails whether the leaders are appointed or elected, and whether they lead in commercial enterprises, governmental organisations or entities within the not-for-profit sector. Is this reflecting the feeling that many contemporary 'leaders' are not visibly demonstrating leadership at all? Or maybe that they are considered to be 'execucrats' – in it for themselves rather than for serving others?

Over the last decade I find myself increasingly supporting employees to perform effectively in an environment where the biggest obstacle to their success is the lack of support from their manager and/or the senior management structure above them. It is a basic rule of management – if you want loyalty, back your people. Ineffective support and inauthentic leadership are both aspects of the gradual but persistent decline I've noticed in the level of employee confidence in senior managers. My own perceptions are confirmed by responses in employee opinion surveys and 360 degree feedback processes. In one organisation where investment in leadership development has been almost non-existent for years, confidence has recently dropped dramatically taking with it morale, goodwill and productivity.

Wherever I have worked or consulted, I have noticed some areas where there has been disdain for leadership, but it does feel to me that this is more prevalent in an unstable economy where people have more doubts about their own security. My personal view is that there is a widespread lack of focus on supporting the development of leadership competency at all levels and across all sectors. In order to retrieve the situation, leadership development must become part of long-term capacity-building strategy if our organisations, economy and society are to grow and thrive. (*Drive Performance*)

Where the trust of employees, customers, clients, sponsors, donors, partners, volunteers, or the electorate is missing, it is inevitable that the commitment from these stakeholders will decline.

The need for executive leaders to be authentic, reliable and to behave with integrity has never been higher. The increasing complexities of the technologically driven, ever-changing workplace provide senior people with an opportunity as well as a challenge. For those at the top, being perceived as credible and trustworthy has never been so important or so valuable, but the increased emphasis on transparency and heightened external media focus has increased the likelihood that leaders that break trust will be exposed. (*Craft Brands*)

I work with a variety of commercial businesses, charities,

governmental and not-for-profit organisations, and I observe two quite different internal reactions to the difficulties. Where the top layer of management tightens controls, restricts or censors communication, or are unclear about strategy and direction, employees become confused and concerned, and thus fear and mistrust gain a foothold; 'Radio Corridor' takes over and is the main source of (mis)information.

Conversely then, it would follow that organisations that recognize the need to build high-trust environments will reap the rewards of greater employee engagement with increased effectiveness and productivity. They will also experience stronger teamwork relationships and collaboration across the business, a positive working environment that increases job satisfaction, all contributing to significant improvements in the overall results.

And results are more than just the tangible outputs or the bottom line profitability. Effective working relationships enhance communication within the team that in turn develops innovation and drives up teamwork. These effects are significant business results in their own right. They are the life-blood of a modern organisation – the factor that makes things happen efficiently or stands in the way of getting things done.

When establishing and developing workplace relationships trust is the most significant factor that must be taken care of as it plays a major role in our decision-making process and therefore the judgments that we all make about others. Trust is a two-way process that affects whether others perceive us as competent, well-intentioned, reliable and credible and whether we recognize others the same way. We need to know whether we can trust each other to do what has been agreed; whether we will get the job done according to the time commitments and quality standards; whether intentions are honourable; and whether we can rely on each other to keep a confidence when the situation calls for it. To be perceived as credible takes effort, and requires that we make our intentions towards others and our motives clear.

As an Executive Leader, being thought of as authentic and credible is vital, as this will inspire trust and confidence in you and your message. Others measure us on the gap between what we say and what we do. Perception alone of being trustworthy is not enough. We must demonstrate this through our actions; we must lead by example and model the way forward for our team to adopt. So – are you interested solely in being ***perceived*** as trustworthy, or ***being*** trustworthy? The difference is what will make a difference.

However, your personal reputation alone is not enough – at the executive level you will also be in a position to actively influence and promote an organisational culture of trust and help to create a positive environment within which trust is fostered and developed. You will shape the behaviour choices of the next generation of leaders through the example you present.

It is my firm belief that all these factors create a strategic differential between one organisation and another; or put in another way, these factors should be regarded as an organisational competency. In short, trust transforms organisations. The latest annual survey in a study by Interaction Associates gathered responses from around 400 professionals from 290 companies across the globe. Comparisons of the results between high-performing organisations (HPOs) and low-performing organisations (LPOs) demonstrated a direct link between trust, engagement and company performance. It also showed an increasing realisation by top leaders that trust emanates from them, and that they must do what it takes to model the behaviours that build trust and employee engagement.

WHAT IS TRUST?

Trust is multi-dimensional and comes in different flavours. What I am saying is that we must be aware of the need to build trust in different dimensions. As we discussed earlier, we must understand the types of trust, and work hard to build all of them as they feed and drive each other. It is also vital to comprehend how the interactions of trust (and, indeed, mistrust) in one dimension will affect another.

As an Executive Leader, you must accept that trust starts with confidence and trust in you, your ability to make good decisions, and to demonstrate sound judgment. Operating in any business entity, you will be expected to share responsibility with your leadership team colleagues for ensuring the continued existence of your business or organisation. In order to sustain it successfully you must ensure that your customers, clients, sponsors or donors have confidence that your

Navigate

organisation will meet their needs, deliver the required results *and* that you are more likely than your competitors (or alternative sources) to do this.

Build Trust

This public confidence, or ***market trust***, is generated through the direct experiences your customers, clients, sponsors or donors have with the people, products, services and results delivered by your organisation. It influences, and is in turn influenced by, the reputation and/or brand of your organisation. If these stakeholders doubt that you will fulfil your mandate or deliver the goods, they will look for alternatives or seek guarantees (such as penalty clauses, requiring credentials such as industry accreditations, insurances, or bonds etc.) thereby applying greater pressure on your organisation. Doubts about credibility can result in product recalls, or votes of no confidence by shareholders. Sponsors or shareholders may ask for tighter controls, more detailed reporting, changes of strategy – all of which can be unsettling, further increasing mistrust and fear, with the resultant impact on profitability and/or viability. People act based on their perceptions of reality, rather than reality itself.

There will also be an impact on the long-term relationship between the business and the stakeholders. In uncertain times, could you afford this?

Social media and on-line reputation sites influence the customers' perception of an entity. It is imperative that executive leaders recognise the power of these communities and actively ensure that they use these mechanisms to reassure potential customers that they are dependable and honest. 'Social proof' delivers strong psychological reassurance – "if it's ok for others, then it's probably going to be ok for me."

It would seem reasonable to assume that this applies in the main to on-line businesses, but any business should be aware; even if a business does not have a prominent on-line presence, Twitter can destroy a reputation instantly. Regardless of global presence, tools such as this operate independently of company location. Take, for example, on-line buying sites such as eBay; if the seller provides a bad experience, a customer can give negative feedback or write an unflattering review that could damage the rating of the supplier and impact future sales. Why are social media such as Twitter, Facebook and other online communities so influential? Because the community members trust the people who rate and review the products and services. Indeed, most of my work offers these days come through referrals or recommendations via LinkedIn and my online business network.

Managing the market trust of the brand and the reputation of the organisation on social media has now become an important element in any growth strategy. Executive leaders must understand the impact that the effective use of social media can have on the reputation and image of their organisation (and, therefore, also on market trust) and educate themselves on the effective deployment and monitoring of these tools. (*Craft Brands*)

Whatever the vibe inside an organisation, it will make its way outside into the market. A strong culture of trust, openness and transparency within the organisation has a profound effect on driving market trust.

Build Trust

Internal attitudes and actions inevitably affect the customer edge in a number of tangible and measurable ways (simple or complex systems, proactive or reactive responses to problems, flexible or inflexible procedures, and employee attitudes when engaging the customer). Indeed, an issue that large organisations face is that many employees are far removed from the external customer. In any business or organisation it is key to trust building that all staff recognise their internal colleagues

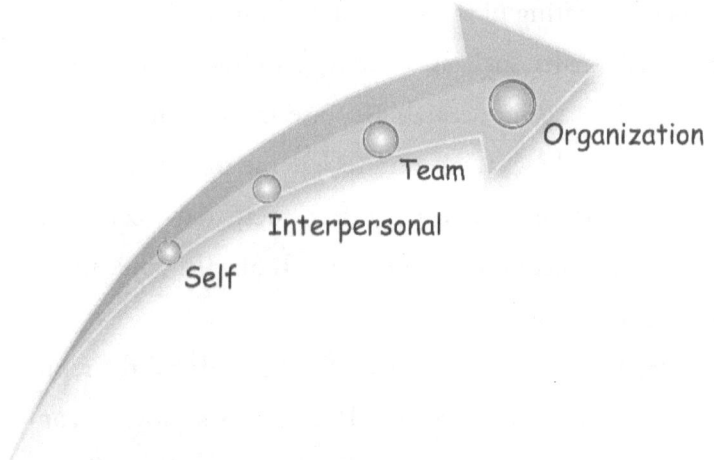

as their customers, and leaders encourage an 'always' attitude to excellent customer service.

High levels of *organisational trust* have knock-on effects inside too, such as less stringent control systems, more authority pushed to lower levels and increased general empowerment of staff to operate autonomously, be free to be creative, to take reasonable risks and make informed decisions. These flexibilities increase employee engagement and collaboration, which in turn affects teamwork, productivity and overall profitability. In non-profit organisations, the results can be measured in terms of greater outcome value delivered to the client or beneficiary.

In an increasingly borderless workplace, teams face more hurdles and obstacles to successful teamwork than ever before. Building and maintaining collaborative relationships should not be left to chance. Working in a way that increases the value of interdependent workplace relationships is just as important as delivering the tasks, and increasingly is being given equal weighting in terms of the importance of outcomes, in enlightened organisations looking to maximize the value of employee effort.

High-performance teams run from a high-trust base. They accept shared responsibility for creating an environment within which they can deliver success. To effect this, they act to minimize the hurdles to developing trust within the team (*team trust*) that emanate from working across technology, distance, language, culture, time zones and business practice.

Without mutual or shared trust, collaborative effort breaks down, and teams suffer from isolation, confusion, and lack of cohesion. As a benchmark test, ask yourself whether you are spending too much time on achieving the task result at the cost of developing and enhancing team trust. The traditional approach is to get to work, and let trust develop as an output. This may work, but in a borderless operating model, this strategy increases the risk.

Interpersonal trust is a natural occurrence between people when each works in a respectful manner, and they treat each other in a fair, open and honest way. On a one-to-one basis, individual actions and attitudes build over time, and we are able to judge each other based on tacit knowledge that we acquire through our daily interactions. It is important, therefore, to be authentic from the start – show others your best self and then act consistently in ongoing dealings. *(Know Yourself)*

HOW DO I DO IT?

If you are going to develop in this area, you will first need to decide to see trust as a 'hard' issue – this means, understand that you will have to consciously work at it, maintain it and regularly measure it. Below, I provide suggestions on immediate actions you can take to start building trust in all the different areas:

START WITH YOU

Your first step is to assess your own attitudes to trust, and how your behaviour toward others supports or hinders the establishment of trust-based relationships. Use the Trust Building Self-Assessment Tool provided in the Models, Tools and Techniques section at the end of this chapter.

BUILD INTERPERSONAL TRUST THROUGH AUTHENTIC LEADERSHIP

A sound basis from which to operate as an executive leader is to be honest and genuine in all your interactions, act with care and consideration for yourself and others, and offer trust to others because, as leaders, our role is to serve others, not to be self-serving. Investing trust in others at the first meeting holds a risk that you may get let down, and this can make us cautious towards others.

This practice has always served me well; I have freely offered trust, and let others earn the distrust (that some have). I believe that this gets the best out of the fence sitters. If we are able to do this, we must also recognize that we must decide not to allow ourselves to be damaged if others abuse our trust.

Indeed, you may hold the view that 'trust has to be earned.' On the other hand, the benefits that 'offering trust to gain trust' brings can far outweigh the risks. If you can also adopt the mindset that you will not allow other peoples' behaviour to affect you negatively, then you mitigate the risk that being let down by one person will limit your future ability to offer trust freely.

When trust has developed, you also have a moral obligation to operate the relationship with integrity and be careful not to abuse or damage it. Do not sit back; keep refining the trust, as trust-based relationships must be maintained to avoid complacency.

BE OPEN AND HONEST

Telling the truth and dealing honestly with people in a respectful and adult manner can enhance and deepen relationships. Trust is a natural element of a close relationship and creates a bond of loyalty.

As an executive leader, make a personal practice of being

open with people about information; give them the good news and the bad news equally openly.

However, there will be times when you are not able to say anything, when you restrict information for sound reasons. In this situation, be honest about the fact that you are not at liberty to discuss the issue but that when you are they will know. Then keep your word. In short, you will be judged not just by ***what*** you say, but ***how*** you go about saying it!

INVEST IN YOUR WORKPLACE RELATIONSHIPS

Acquiring the skills to be able to share your views and opinions, with sensitivity, will generate trusting relationships. We tend to have more trust in people who are able and willing to share their personal experiences, concerns or feelings about a situation, particularly where these characteristics are easily visible to us.

Working to build close relationships with colleagues, clients, and key stakeholders will create a sense of reciprocity – each person becoming more likely to support the other and feel a sense of 'being on the same team' and obligation toward them.

High trust relationships are very influential in business, but they must be handled with care and operated with integrity. When trust is broken, it is very difficult to rebuild. (*Make Connections*)

BUILD YOUR PERSONAL CREDIBILITY

People trust others that they perceive as credible. Credibility is our golden gift to ourselves – no one else can give it to us, and no one else can do it as much damage as we are able to do ourselves.

Credibility emanates from two things matching in the minds of others – what we say and what we so. If you make a commitment, keep it. If you advocate a value, act in accordance with it. If you expect certain behaviour from others, demonstrate the behaviour yourself. Act as you want to be perceived and others will copy. By visibly and consistently acting in accordance with corporate values, you will set an example for others, and influence the whole culture of the organisation.

DEMONSTRATE YOUR COMPETENCE

When people in your workplace network know what you are able to do, and have experience of your competence, they will trust you to be able to repeat it. It is necessary that you operate at your highest level of competency. Consistently delivering to a high standard in your key areas of knowledge or skills fosters belief in your abilities and confirms your reputation as a high performer.

CREATE YOUR OWN TRACK RECORD

It is vitally important to be credible by aligning your words and actions, and meeting your commitments. It is also important to be viewed as reliable by acting consistently and delivering to others' expectations; both contribute to your track record and enhance your reputation.

Nevertheless, you can give trust a further boost by subtly

Build Trust

taking action to increase your visibility, gently mentioning your successes and achievements and promoting your positive reputation. Successful executive leaders look after their personal brand, without coming across as arrogant. Look for opportunities to use personal examples of success such as recommendations, referrals, case studies, or testimonials, especially with new contacts that may need you to establish some credentials. (*Craft Brands*)

DEMONSTRATE RELIABILITY

Being reliable is another route to creating trust. Along with credibility, reliability is generated through the frequency of interactions. The more you work with someone, the more the other person will understand how you operate and whether you are consistent in fulfilling his or her needs and expectations. Get to know your key contacts and their working preferences and style; deliver with consistency. The more experience they have of you, the more reliable they will judge you to be. Make time to meet with the relevant people in your network, adding to their tacit knowledge of you over time by ensuring some frequency of contact – the more that they get to know you, the more their confidence in you will build bit by bit, adding goodwill into a goodwill account.

SHOW EMPATHY

Learn how to demonstrate empathy when others may feel uncertain and vulnerable, or when discussing sensitive matters. This will help to reassure others that you are supportive of them. Don't back away from discussing the tough stuff; this shows that you care and that it matters to you.

CLEAN UP AFTER YOURSELF

All of us have experienced times when things don't go according to plan, and we have all mucked up occasionally. But how do you handle the effect on others when you make a mistake or muck up? It is inevitable that you will make mistakes occasionally. Ignoring the issue or attempting to hide it will not help your reputation and could damage the trust between you and your colleague or client. Just as my parents used to say to me, "You broke it, you fix it."

Admitting the mistake as early as possible, then taking action quickly to mitigate or minimize the impact to colleagues or clients is vital. Taking positive steps to set things right, get things back on track with a clear plan of action and regular communication will preserve the trust between you, protect the relationship and show that you take your commitments seriously.

This attitude needs to permeate the whole business, especially at the sharp end where your front line people interact with the client or customer. Executive leaders have a responsibility to promote a culture where it is safe to admit mistakes, and where employees are empowered to make it right.

BUILD TRUST IN TEAMS THROUGH COACHING

Whilst many teams expect trust to develop naturally through the act of working together, this is an unsafe strategy akin to keeping one's fingers crossed and hoping it all works out. Key to successfully building trust within a team is to explicitly discuss the issue early, and often.

Coach and educate your team about trust – hold everyone responsible for the quality of their workplace relationships. Facilitate team values and team rules. Have colleagues hold each other to account for observing the rules, and managing conflict constructively.

Model the attitudes that you expect by building healthy relationships with your top team colleagues and partnering with your direct reports. Build openness and honesty into the recruitment and selection profiles for your team. Ensure that team members are coached in collaborative working especially when they are working with virtual and remote team members.

BUILD A HIGH-TRUST ORGANISATION

Build high levels of trust throughout the whole organisation by developing a trust-building strategy and driving it from the top. Work with other senior leaders to craft a plan for a high-trust culture. Establish corporate values that embrace honesty, integrity, and respect and jointly commit to demonstrable behaviours that model these values. Build the values into the performance management processes by defining specific demonstrable behaviours within a competency model. (*Drive Performance*) Ensure that the demonstration of corporate values is recognized and rewarded. Deal swiftly with behaviours that work against the values.

Conduct organisation-wide trust surveys to get feedback and identify issues. Take action to address the issues (real and perceived) such as organising facilitated workshops on the subject, to foster involvement, generate ideas, and mobilize staff effort at the local level.

Publish an action plan with a balanced scorecard approach to measuring both the quantitative and qualitative elements. This method can also be used to transform a low trust team to a high trust one. Create milestones, and measure improvements in perceptions as well as tangible effects.

CREATE TRUST WITH YOUR CUSTOMERS TO BUILD REPUTATION

Ensure that the key objectives of the business include the creation of market trust and link this to the bottom line. A confident and loyal customer base brings measurable economic benefits to the business that can and should be tracked and reported.

Invest in educating all customer-facing staff (whether serving internal or external customers) in the importance of integrity and honesty. Ensure they understand and demonstrate the organisational values, and regard themselves as the trust custodians of the organisation. Provide training and support for them to acquire the behavioural competencies and interpersonal skills as well as the technical competence and product knowledge to provide first-class service.

Manage your market reputation through listening to the customer using direct methods, but more increasingly via social networking tools. Engage in dialogue with your customers through robust customer feedback mechanisms, and visibly act on feedback. Make it as easy as possible for them to talk to you and to do business with you. Show them that you want to listen to what they have to say.

It is worth recognizing that there has been a recent shift away from using high 'would-refer' scores as a measurement of excellence in customer service, to using high 'ease-of-use' scores. In short, customers are telling us that they want to do business with organisations that make it easy for them to do business with them.

WHAT IF I DON'T BUILD TRUST?

Can your business afford a low-trust culture? Where trust is absent, mistrust takes its place. Low-trust behaviours are tolerated and allowed to become successful. Negative behaviours are accepted as 'the way to get on around here' and copied. People become fearful; communication suffers, control mechanisms become tighter, productivity drops along with morale and employee engagement. What flows from the inside out will also affect your organisation from the outside back in, as market trust erodes, and customer / sponsor goodwill diminishes. The effect on your bottom line will be dramatic.

MODELS, TOOLS AND TECHNIQUES

You can use our Trust Building Self-Assessment Tool to understand your ability to build trust-based workplace relationships. Assess each of the questions by considering the extent to which your behaviour meets that suggested by the question. In the 'Action' column note any action you will take to either improve or maintain your effectiveness.

Navigate

TRUST BUILDING SELF-ASSESSMENT TOOL

Go through the questions and for each one ask, what one action will I take to address my answer.

QUESTIONS

1. Are you honest and genuine in all your interactions?
2. Do you act with care and consideration for yourself and others at all times?
3. Do you freely offer trust to others?
4. Do you operate your relationships with integrity, being careful not to abuse or damage them?
5. Do you avoid complacency by acting to refine the trust in your relationships?
6. Do you make a personal practice of being open and honest with people at all times?
7. Do you invest in your workplace relationships by sharing your personal experiences, concerns or feelings about situations, building collaborative working relationships and generating a sense of reciprocity?
8. Do you build your personal credibility by acting in accordance with your spoken values, meeting your commitments and modelling the behaviours you expect from others?
9. Do you demonstrate your competence by delivering to a high standard in your key areas of knowledge or skills?
10. Do you create your own track record by increasing your visibility, mentioning your achievements and promoting your positive reputation?

11. Do you demonstrate your reliability to others and by doing so grow their goodwill and confidence in you?
12. Do you demonstrate empathy when others feel uncertain and vulnerable, or when discussing sensitive matters?
13. Do you clean up after yourself, admitting your mistakes and taking action to minimize any impact on others?

OTHER TRUST ASSESSMENTS, SURVEYS AND AUDITS

As you attain an executive role, you could initiate the use of internal organisation-wide assessments of trust and/or surveys of trust in the organisation as seen through the eyes of your customers. A simple internet search of the words 'trust survey' will bring you a plethora of suggestions for questions and how to measure the results. Alternatively, you could include the questions in a wider employee satisfaction survey, or customer/market survey.

POINTS OF INTEREST

Some of the key facets in this chapter include:

- **What is trust?** We explore the nature of trust and individual attitudes towards it; we examine different forms of trust and the effect that it has at every level of the organisation, from trust in self, to trust between peers, within and between teams, and across the organisation. The inside-out nature of trust is reflected, therefore, in market trust – do your customers trust you enough to do business with you? *How aware are you about how trust* *affects your relationships, and how it affects relationships at all levels in your organisation?*

- **The importance of building trust:** To build positive, productive performance at all levels it is incumbent upon the senior leadership to sponsor and strengthen trust-based relationships and communication from the inside out, if the business is to be trusted by customers and the marketplace. How will you take action to sponsor and reinforce trust-based relationships within your organisation?

- **Creating a high-trust organisation:** Executive Leaders who place trust building high on their list of priorities model the behaviour they expect from others and actively invest time and money in organisation-wide trust building initiatives. These executive actions are not only being rewarded by quantifiable bottom-line benefits, but they also foster an environment within which employee engagement, job satisfaction and quality of relationships all improve. What can you do to generate initiatives that support the creation of a high-trust organisation and how will you know that these have been successful?

Remember as you read through the chapter to reflect on the questions asked, note what comes up in your journal. Use the resources we have made available to you to check and assess where you are. Following reflection, witness what comes up for you and make a note of that and any actions required.

Build Trust

TAKING STOCK

Taking Stock

You have now completed the first eight points of the Executive Leadership Compass. Take time now to reflect on the impact that these chapters have had on you.

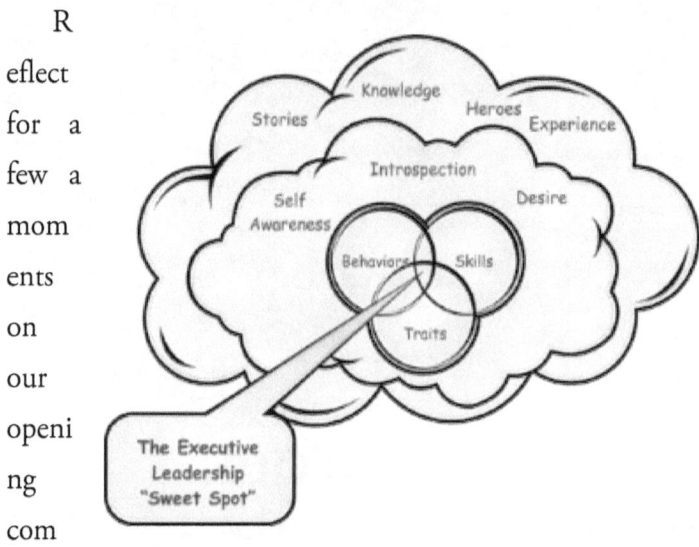

Reflect for a few moments on our opening comments. In order to first, even have the desire to craft ourselves in some purposeful way, and then to determine the appropriate courses of action to take, requires a combination of introspection, self-awareness and desire.

Have you been using the Executive Leadership Compass, The Roadmap to Executive Leadership Success and your Executive Leadership Journal? How have they helped you? How could you use them to help spur your introspection, to foster your insights, and further fuel your desire?

Now prepare for further adventure, learning, and growth with Part 2 of The Executive Leadership Journey, where you will complete your guided tour of the remaining eight points of the Executive Leadership Compass.

ABOUT THE AUTHORS

"The whole is greater than the sum of its parts"

Anon

About The Authors
THE AUTHORS' VOICE

Having a book written by four authors who passionately believe that Executive Leadership is a unique, exciting and often challenging journey, but one that is immensely fulfilling when in the right environment and aligned to your values, passion and purpose.

Each has worked in senior roles and has developed and delivered executive training and coaching. We have each, first, walked the walk of Executive Leadership. Only then did we each commit to helping others with similar journeys. We first came together as a team of four due to shared experiences with a common client, Learning Tree International. From that shared experience we committed to combining our experiences, insights and voices for the benefit of others sharing similar journeys.

We know that each and every one of you has a unique voice and to increase the probability that you will connect with one or more of us, we have made a deliberate choice to keep our individual voices in each of our chapters. In doing so, we have incorporated insights from each of the other authors, weaving the chapters together for consistency and clarity.

We trust that you will enjoy engaging with each of us, both individually and as a team of four, along your journey. Our desire is to share some of our insights and understandings, and to encourage you to take the elements that most resonate with you, to create your own Executive Leadership roadmap for success.

CASEY KROLL

Casey Kroll has over 20 years of General Management (Managing Director) experience, with strengths in the areas of business re-invention, business development, project and program management, engineering and marketing. His desire to help his clients benefit from his wealth of experience led him to create Etra, Inc., a private consultancy focused on helping clients (both organisations and individuals) develop a leadership direction, and on helping these clients implement their vision.

He holds both Bachelors and Masters of Science in Engineering, and an MBA. He has achieved certification as a Project Management Professional (PMP) by the Project Management Institute, and has a Green Belt from ITT's renowned Lean 6 Sigma program. Casey has worked with large publically-traded corporations, privately held businesses, not-for-profit organisations, government agencies and select individuals.

JUDI WILLIAMS

Judi Williams runs an award-winning company called Great Beginnings, which designs and delivers training in all aspects of behavioural competencies and performance in the workplace. With over 30 years' experience in business leadership and management, Judi specialises in personal and team performance at the Executive Leadership level, and holds an Advanced Diploma in Executive Coaching. She provides executive coaching services and custom designed learning solutions, working directly with clients and through

About The Authors

commercial training companies.

Judi is passionate about people, and is dedicated to supporting them to be their best in whatever they do. To support the unlocking of potential Great Beginnings offers a variety of routes to personal change – one-on-one or team coaching, NLP techniques, life coaching and hypnotherapy. Judi operates globally, and serves a wide range of clients in throughout Europe, North America and the Middle East.

RAHUL DOGRA

Rahul Dogra has over twenty years of senior management experience in running an international software company and has extensively worked with a number of industries including consultancy and engineering (water, aeronautical and mechanical).

Rahul has created and delivered a range of management courses throughout Europe, Africa, Middle East and North America. He has developed and delivered programs on global teams, cultural awareness, business ethics and performance enhancement within organisations. Clients include Emerson, Logica, Accenture, Citibank and GE.

Rahul runs a software company and draws on his practical business expertise combined with his formal academic MBA to continually enhance the organisation's performance. Rahul has also enjoyed a second career as a facilitated trainer and enjoys working with international clients with diverse teams. He has also lectured in an academic environment at MBA level, tutoring students across Europe and in Oman.

DALE DARLEY

Dale Darley started her career in software, teaching accountants how to use software. It created a passion for software and systems as enablers for change and for supporting growth.

The journey, for all careers, are journeys, has taken her from training, through pre-sales, account management, new business sales, onto marketing / personal branding and writing. Throughout the whole journey, she has written – books, copy, articles, blogs and stories.

An MBA kick-started a new quest for learning, and she has been on a journey of discovery ever since. Sitting through a gruelling leadership development programme awakened her curiosity to the way in which people communicate. After passing her ILM level 7 executive coaching certificate, life came full circle, and she could see how to focus her love of stories and the written word alongside coaching and training.

Dale works with clients to discover what they want to write about, helps them to plan, write, edit, and self publish their books.

Dale's own books are primarily self-development, where she uses her life and business experiences to pull together content which is useful, simple, practical and life-changing.

She believes that writing heals and indeed many of her clients come to her to write business books, only to discover that there are elements of their life meandering through the themes that need clarity. She works to help them overcome any stumbling blocks and find a way to heal these through their writing or via other means.

BIBLIOGRAPHY

Bibliography

PLAN JOURNEYS

Carroll, Louis G. *Alice's Adventures in Wonderland* (commonly shortened to *Alice in Wonderland*) London: Macmillan, 1865.

Southey, Robert. "The Story of the Three Bears". *The Doctor*. London: Longman, Rees, 1837.

KNOW YOURSELF

Brown, Brené. The Gifts of Imperfection: Let Go of Who You Think You're Supposed to Be and Embrace Who You Are. Center City, MN: Hazelden, 2010.

Cashman, Kevin. *Leadership from the Inside Out: Becoming a Leader for Life*. San Franciso, CA: Berrett-Kohler Publishers, 2008.

Covey, Stephen R. *Principle-Centered Leadership*. London: Simon & Schuster, 1999.

Dilts, Robert. Changing Belief Systems with Neuro-Linguistic Programming [NLP]. Capitola, CA: Meta Publications, 1990.

    Dylan, Bob, American folksinger, b. 1941

    Eliot, George, Novelist, b. Mary An Evans 1819

    Shakespeare, William. *Hamlet*.

Whitmore, John. Coaching for Performance: Growing Human Potential and Purpose - The Principles and Practice of Coaching and Leadership. London: Nicholas Brealey Publishing, 2009.

UNDERSTAND THE BUSINESS

Collins, Jim. *Good to Great: Why Some Companies Make the Leap...And Others Don't*. New York: Harper Collins, 2001.

Tropman, John E. and Lynn Wooten. "Executive Leadership: A 7C Approach". *Problems and Perspectives in Management* 8 no. 4 (2010): 47-57.

Waterman, Robert H. Jr., Thomas J. Peters and Julien R. Phillips. "Structure Is Not Organization". *Business Horizons* (June 1980): 14-26.

CREATE VISION

Covey, Stephen R. *The Seven Habits of Highly Effective People*. Philadelphia: Running Press, 2000.

Inglis, Scott. *Making the Most of Action Learning*. Aldershot: Gower, 1994.

STRIKE BALANCES

Branson, Richard. Interview with Neil Duffy (Chairman and Founder of Tribe Management for Real Leaders), accessed 14/4/2014 http://real-leaders.com/richard-branson-reinventing-how-we-live-and-work/

Collins, Jim. *Good to Great: Why Some Companies Make the Leap...And Others Don't*. New York: Harper Collins, 2001.

LEAD STRATEGIES

Collins, Jim. *Good to Great: Why Some Companies Make the Leap...And Others Don't*. New York: Harper Collins, 2001.

Porter, M. E. "How Competitive Forces Shape Strategy". *Harvard Business Review* 57 no. 2 (March–April 1979): 137–145.

MAKE CONNECTIONS

Pink, Daniel H. To sell is Human – The Surprising Truth About Persuading, Convincing and Influencing Others. Edinburgh: Canongate Books, 2013. ISBN: 978 0 85786 719 3

BUILD TRUST

Jobs, Steven Paul, Chairman and CEO of Apple Inc. Address at Stanford University, 2005.

Schneier, Bruce. Liars and Outliers: Enabling the Trust that Society Needs to Survive. Indianapolis, IN: John Wiley & Sons, 2012.

www.ingramcontent.com/pod-product-compliance
Lightning Source LLC
Chambersburg PA
CBHW020909180526
45163CB00007B/2686